About the Author

Born and raised in Caracas, Venezuela, where I got an MD degree, culminating post-graduate studies in Cambridge, Mexico City, Houston, Chapel Hill, and New York in the fields of Pediatric and Adult Neurology. Experiences as lay missionary in South America, China, Pakistan, and Africa were responsible for my comprehensive actual approach in the practice of medicine.

Missionary Without a Mission

Enrique A. Wulff

Missionary Without a Mission

Vanguard Press

VANGUARD PAPERBACK

© Copyright 2024
Enrique A. Wulff

The right of Enrique A. Wulff to be identified as author of this work has been asserted by him in accordance with the Copyright, Designs and Patents Act 1988.

All Rights Reserved

No reproduction, copy or transmission of this publication may be made without written permission.
No paragraph of this publication may be reproduced, copied or transmitted save with the written permission of the publisher, or in accordance with the provisions of the Copyright Act 1956 (as amended).

Any person who commits any unauthorised act in relation to this publication may be liable to criminal prosecution and civil claims for damages.

A CIP catalogue record for this title is available from the British Library.

ISBN 978 1 83794 016 5

Vanguard Press is an imprint of
Pegasus Elliot Mackenzie Publishers Ltd.
www.pegasuspublishers.com

First Published in 2024

Vanguard Press
Sheraton House Castle Park
Cambridge England

Printed & Bound in Great Britain

Missionary Without a Mission is specially dedicated to the person who is reading the book

To everyone who was involved in any one of the
missionary adventures mentioned in the book

Missionary Without a Mission is the product of a strange awakening without knowing that one is waking up. It is a story and it is a retelling. It is something that will slide like a story during the moments I tell it to you. It is an experience, it is an existence, it is a living, it is an existing... that deals with what has gone, what is and what potentially will be.

Everything that, in the linearity that we experience our existence, belongs to what we know as the past and that we believe is already gone, that it will not return, that is forgotten and that is only remembered at the discretion of our memories and our emotional selections of them... it will gradually be outlined, as the memories make their way between the words.

This attempt to try to bring up what was left behind in the walk, is with the only idea of creating a sequence. A sequence for the reader. At this point in my life, there are no more sequences – everything is part of everything. What was my past, what is my present and what will be my future are mixed in me, like the ingredients of a soup. I have called that soup my conscience. In this soup of my conscious life, the variables, time, space and gravity seem not to identify with each other. Perhaps this is why I feel my inner voice telling me that I always am, regardless of what my conscience believes.

This manuscript may perhaps become a book. This depends on how synchronous, efficient and engaged my mind, my feelings and my emotions are, when they begin to be seen themselves in the reflection of the words.

This book is already written, I am just remembering it with you. At what moment it began to be written, is what I am not very clear about. I remember witnessing intentions, expectations, possibilities that were taking shape in the world of extraordinary circumstances, and over time my life was losing its simplicity, being unable to control my conscious and perhaps subconscious restlessness, which only wanted a complicated life.

My simple life was like sitting in a train car, moving through the prairies. My restlessness made the train leave the prairies to enter the mountains, having no idea that those mountains were roller coasters.

In the ravages of leaving an adolescence to explore what it is to be an adult, the natural ups and downs of life began to acquire intensity, generating periods of turbulence that subsided in ephemeral sensations of calm, amid illusions, passions, joys, and sadness. The "tremendousness" of childhood quickly turned into adventures. My thoughts, feelings, actions and words changed so quickly that the only way to survive was by hiding behind my personality and my character.

There was only one north in my life, and that was what my passion indicated to me. My passion has been and is my greatest propulsor. My passion does not know how to discriminate, which makes me enjoy the most insignificant events, even those that go beyond imagination.

The game of opportunities, the vocation, the circumstances, the inclinations and a fantastic idea of a potential reality… they placed in my hands a passport, in which could be read on its cover "Medical Doctor and Surgeon." At the time, when I was twenty-three years old, I had no idea what this passport meant, let alone how far it would allow me to explore the dimensions of love and human pain.

My first medical diagnosis, within minutes of having this passport in my hands, was the realization that the beginning was over and that what continued was not found in what I knew. A strange feeling of security drove me towards the insecurity of exploring the unknown, and in hours, the commitments made with a view to a successful, productive and fruitful future in the arts of practicing medicine in my country, dissolved into nothingness, unknowingly opening the doors to an adventure.

The traditional and conventional were left behind, as I flew to London. My landing on the realities stole my breath and verbal expression from my mind, my emotions and my feelings. For a reasonable enough time, I felt like Tarzan, not because I was in a jungle, but because I spoke English like him.

I quickly learned that a language is not mastered through study alone. My ignorance created the false illusion that by studying fourteen to sixteen hours a day – as I used to do during my medical career – I would be able to master the art of communicating my thoughts and feelings in the English language. And to reconfirm my illusory ignorance, my dyslexia, which I managed to survive during the years I spent at La Salle School and at the university, decided to make itself known in my existence, with all the radiance of its nature and essence.

For many months, I felt what it really is to be anonymous. All kinds of anecdotes were generated in this surviving in a language other than mine. Some made me laugh, and many others made me cry.

The body language in the winter of England did not help much in my communication with the outside world. I felt like a kindergartener again – moving around on a bicycle and learning to speak, read and write.

Studying medicine in Venezuela, for me, did not follow the uniqueness and dedication that it deserved by its nature and essence. Existential circumstances and needs led me to work in areas not associated with medicine. I worked as a substitute teacher in mathematics, physics and biology in private schools and high schools during the day, alternating with medical school, and at night I taught in higher education institutes for adults, where the bachelor's degree in science was awarded after two years of intensive studies.

In one of these adult education institutes, I learned about the importance of paying attention to what was learned or instilled in me, so as not to harm anyone. One night, a student in his forties interrupted a Physics class when I was explaining the development of a complex problem, telling me that I did not need to humiliate them.

Of course, I got a little messed up by this unexpected statement. And I asked what he was referring to.

He replied, "You have asked more than five to six times if we understand, and that made us feel that we were less intelligent than you…"

From that moment to the present, when I explain something, I say: "Do I explain myself clear enough?" and "Did I make myself understood?" and no longer, "Do you understand me?"

Also, life during my years of study at the medical school placed me in situations where they helped me deal with unfounded fears. One of them was working in the Model Prison in the city of Caracas, where there were inmates with long sentences. I went there two nights a week. I got in at six p.m., and I remained locked up in jail until six a.m. the next day. Regardless of dealing with the aforementioned fears, it was very positive for me, since it allowed me to spend several hours studying, and above all, it gave me the opportunity to establish friendships with many of the inmates, some for their visits as patients in the infirmary, and others that I visited in their cells.

The idea of practicing medicine ranged from my innocent desire to do it in a specific area, to end up doing it in what I wanted. But it was not that simple. During my medical career, I began to identify the areas in which I did not feel comfortable, and through this discard I tried to identify the area in which I would like to work in my years of professional practice. Two areas were ruled out in the first contacts with them. These were neurology and geriatrics. And following this process of likes and discards, by the last year of the medical school, I already knew that I wanted to be a pediatrician. With the idea of pediatrics in my mind and in my heart, I launched into the world in its conquest.

I wanted to be the best pediatrician that my abilities could lead me to be. I began the specialization in this area of medicine at Addenbrooke's Hospital in Cambridge, to continue it at the DIF Pediatric Hospital in the south of Mexico City and finished it at the Children's Hospital of Mexico. After submitting the thesis and passing the corresponding oral exams, I was accredited by the Academy of Pediatrics of Mexico.

A few months before finishing my pediatric residency in Mexico, the opportunity to continue my postgraduate studies in the USA presented itself.

I was already twenty-eight years old, but the passion and the spirit of adventure did not grow old with me. On the contrary, they were increasing, with greater intention and strength.

The director of the Department of Pathology and the specialist in Pediatric Neuropathology at Hospital Infantil de México, arranged an interview for me on January 4 at the Houston Medical Center at the hospitals affiliated with the University of Texas.

I remember that I borrowed winter clothes, and I went to the interview without knowing for sure what an interview was like, to apply for a resident position in a hospital in the USA. I remember arriving in heavy winter clothes and a woolen scarf. The outside temperature in Houston was around 1-2 degrees Celsius. Walking from the hotel to the hospital in the cold was fabulous, but when I entered the hospital, I did not count on the heating. In order not to lose the elegance with which I prepared myself, I kept all those clothes on until the moment of the interview. Of course, I was sweating like a chicken on embers, not only because of the heat, but because of how nervous I was and for the whirlwinds of emotions that were flooding me.

When the head of the Department of Pediatric Neurology began to speak, I did not understand anything he was saying. The little English that I had learned four years ago in England was so hidden in my mind, that I could not find but a few words for courteous England-style communication. So it was the face that I had that he asked me if I was feeling well.

At that moment, the divinity of creation illuminated me almost miraculously, and I managed, with body language mainly and some mispronounced words at will, to say with conviction: "I had severe acute pharyngitis," and between the benevolence and good intention of this extraordinary professor, I managed to spend my day of interviews, in which two more professors interviewed me, the head of the residents and I participated in case presentations with the entire Department of Neurology.

I think that was my first crash course on the relativity of time – the minutes were hours, and the hours felt like days.

Upon my return to Mexico, I told the Director of Pathology of the Children's Hospital what had happened to me. After the expected corresponding healthy laughs and teases of imagining seeing me in the middle of all this and knowing that I had no idea of what they said to me, she agreed to call the professor in Houston to ask him how my interview had been.

In short, I had to pass the medical exams to be recognized as a US doctor (ECFMG) and to obtain the visa that would allow me to stay doing a postgraduate residency in the USA (Visa Qualifying Examination –VQE).

Two months later, I began to make rounds to patients from the hospitals affiliated with Baylor College of Medicine of the same Houston Medical Center, with a neurologist and his associate, who taught me quality in the art of practicing neurology in adults, where humanism, compassion and benevolence set the tone. They were eighteen months of "quality in time." During those eighteen months, I presented and passed the aforementioned exams.

This neurologist was of Mexican origin, and I enjoyed everything Mexican much more with him than in the three and a half years I had spent in Mexico City.

Because of this, my English did not improve as expected, and I began my postgraduate residency in pediatric neurology understanding about forty percent of what they told me. Thank God I had learned the ways and details in the previous eighteen months of patient management.

I will always be grateful to all the doctors who had to fight with the frustrations that my dyslexia and little knowledge of English generated. For them it was my accent and my limited capacity for written expression, but the secret of the true truth had to stay with me, since their minds could not handle the harsh reality. Also, they would never have accepted me in such a prestigious program.

As you can see, what I did not like in the medical school began to manifest in my realities, and little by little I got involved in the field of neurology. Life, throughout its earthly time in me, has led me to experience other things in relation to medicine. For example: after five years of postgraduate studies in pediatrics, the opportunity to exercise it never presented itself. After completing the specialization in pediatric neurology in Houston and in Chapel Hill, North Carolina, and being recognized by the American Board of the specialty, I did not manage, until sixteen years later, to practice pediatric neurology for two years in Pensacola and Gulf Breeze, Florida, thanks to having finished my neurology residency at the University of South Florida in Tampa. Being certified by the American Board of Neurology and Psychiatry allowed me, from time to time and from moment to moment, to have had the opportunity to practice general neurology over the years and in many parts of the world. A new subspecialty in neurological complications of HIV and AIDS, carried out at the Mount Sinai Medical Center in Manhattan, NY, in the late 'nineties, for my reincorporation to neurological medicine in North America, also did not have the opportunity to be practiced. In the last eight years, I have been working in the field of geriatric neurology in Miami, Florida.

The search for American citizenship for me and my family, and its passage through different types of visas with the mandatory requirements involved in them, played a fundamental role in what was mentioned in the previous paragraph.

And to finish this topic, I tell you that working in the field of geriatric neurology is what I most want to do. For me it is not a job, but an opportunity to learn and share with the experience, with the physical and mental designs of age, with tradition, with life, with spirituality and with death.

And so, the first thing that was discarded while I was beginning my first steps in the field of medicine is what marked and marks my professional practice of it. The illusion of preparing and specializing in prestigious universities and hospitals around the world and to return to Venezuela and be able to offer my expertise in the medical area to my country of origin, was truncated to an intermittent, temporary, and in dribs and drabs medical activity.

This allowed me to change from Venezuelan citizen to a citizen of the world, and then to an American citizen, but with my conscience, my mind, my thinking, my feeling, my acting and my speaking, working in the global concept of humanity and not in the individual concept of a citizenship.

At the present time, I am as American as Venezuelan, and a citizen of the place in the world where I find myself.

In a way, the "Medical Doctor and Surgeon" passport that was granted to me in Venezuela led me to experience the metamorphosis of caterpillar-cocoon-butterfly on several occasions throughout my life.

My caterpillar moments taught me that there is no difference between any of the human beings who experience different realities throughout the Earth. We are all spiritual entities that are part of the whole of the divinity of creation, living an experience in a dense dimension for the benefit and learning of the unity of the everything and of the nothing.

My cocoon moments helped me to know the fragility of life, the meaning of my personality and of my character in my manifestation as part of humanity; to know who I am, where I come from, where I am and where I am going. It sensitized me to learn to be aware of my conscience and of the conscience of others in the midst of the respect for the individuality of the diversity, as well as the right to have the freedom to exercise my free will authentically, without fear and without pressure.

And my butterfly moments, where, thank God, I find myself experiencing in these moments, bless me daily with the opportunity to enjoy the intelligent and beautiful nature that involves the concept of Mother Earth, making me experience much more, day by day, of the limited concept of Heaven, with the opportunity to fall in love with my own divinity and with the divinity of living beings that I meet daily. With the opportunity to feel happiness in the joy of living and in the satisfaction of dying; with the opportunity to experience, in my consciousness the cyclical-undulating meaning of life, its actions and reactions, as well as the essence of unity between the macrocosm of the universe and the microcosm of my human manifestation.

Now I know that I am energy, an energy that is part of the divinity and of the love of what the concept of God represents for humanity. An energy that moves in an undulating way between light and darkness, between the divine and the human, between what we call good and what we call bad, between what we know as joy and what we know as sadness, between abundance and scarcity, between health and illness, between reason and emotion; without ceasing to be what I really am at any time, with the aggravation of acquiring more wisdom and experiencing more love in each undulation.

South America

Influenced by Catholic and Hindu nuns in the early '90s, I accepted the opportunity presented to me to directly help very poor communities. The idea was based on the construction of a basic health center, where natural products that could be obtained directly from nature to its surroundings were used to treat physical and emotional ailments.

The emotion that flooded me in the moment, which prompted me to accept the idea so quickly, began, within hours, its expected forced landing into reality.

I avoided, at first, allowing reason to confuse me, and I dedicated myself, as soon as I could, to diving into the libraries to obtain as much information as possible on alternative medicine and naturism. For several weeks, I studied between fourteen and sixteen hours a day about Asian culture, Ayurvedic medicine, gurus, acupuncture through finger pressure, healing massages, native Indian remedies, etc.

I was literally becoming a homeopathic and naturopathic physician. I tried, as best I could, to interweave the new information with the experiences previously obtained from allopathic medicine, mainly in the areas of pediatrics, internal medicine and neurology.

Do not think that this was as easy as it sounds in the written words. This was literally a sequence of mental, existential, emotional and professional storms.

The Catholic-Hindu organization that I would go to work with in Brazil had quite peculiar existential-spiritual-religious requirements, in which detachment played a primary role.

They started giving me the information directly. I felt it a litany of instructions, given without much subtlety, as people say: "Without mincing the words." They explained to me, that before I started working for the organization, I had to get rid of any material attachments, such as housing, debts, furniture, extra clothes, etc.

That is to say, they asked me to leave behind all the material things and all the things that could somehow link me to my past.

At that time in my life, I was neither very cultured nor aware of the oriental religious-spiritual cultures, which practiced detachment as a very effective way of getting closer to the essence of God and the universe that lives within us.

The detachment that they demanded of me was obviously much more than a simple detachment for me. It was to leave products of my work, commitments, material elements that were part of my life and that filled me with joy when using them.

In those moments, reason and intelligence drew their claws to generate all kinds of emotions to calm the intention and modify the thought. For a few days, it seemed that they were winning the battle, until the famous intuition, with its unique ability in me, managed to blindfold me while it hypnotized me by asking me to walk blindly and that it was going to guide me.

Now that I am writing this, no matter how open-mindedly I wanted to see these moments of my life, I cannot specify or understand much of what kind of thoughts, feelings and emotions I was experiencing, so that they would have had the ability to polarize themselves into actions. I have no doubt that I was walking on a very fine and fragile line that was demarcated between madness, self-suicide, fanciful adventure, despair and the delusional illusion of helping the poor.

It seemed that life was giving me the opportunity to launch myself to explore the unknown with the same passion with which I had been doing it with the known.

What sounds quite paradoxical is that I was doing all this voluntarily, in full consciousness of freedom of my free will.

In those moments, walking became my friend, my counselor and perhaps even my psychological therapist. I remember walking for many hours at a time and for many days, trying to clear my mind and find a balance between my reason, my intelligence, my adventurous spirit, my passion for medicine, my concern to help the needy, and my temporary insanity.

I was beginning to experience what many years later I knew as the strength and power of intuition, the divinity involved in intention, and the divine wisdom implicit in love in action.

It seemed that, despite being in my thirties by that time, I was experiencing the famous 40's crisis (midlife crisis).

In those days, between my conscience, my unconsciousness and my vivid dreams, I made the decision to launch myself into the adventure. I woke up one morning with the conviction that the only way to find out what all these new events were about in my life, was to commit myself with passion and one hundred percent of my thinking, my feeling, my actions and my speech with all that this implied and let myself flow through the unfolding of events.

Getting rid of my material belongings was easier and faster than I thought. I even felt pretty good in the process. Having twelve siblings made it easier for the vast majority of things to disappear in hours.

Throughout this process of transformation and reinvention, an extraordinary human being appeared, of those who manifest themselves in your life so that you know the value of love in friendship, with intelligence, with a constancy in time and an unique commitment. She was demonstrating, day by day, her human-spiritual condition and acted as my protective angel, masterfully coordinating not only the transition, but also preparing the logistics of the potential necessary things that I had to take with me. Without this angel, I don't think I would have managed to get on track with the speed and safety as I did.

This experience of affirmation of friendship left me with a tranquility and a feeling of security, which helped me overcome the many bumps of the road, filling me with a force of hope, which manifested itself as a light in moments of darkness.

For this adventure, I got a 4x4 pickup truck covered with a cab. The rear cabin was filled with medicines and the rest of my things that I found useful for the trip. In the driver's cab, as travel companions, were maps of Venezuela and Brazil, a book on how to learn to speak Portuguese, written in English, clothes to change, a pillow, insecticides, flashlights, a box with tools, mechanics books, two compasses, blankets and a sleeping bag.

Things were fitting in such a way that sooner, rather than later, I was ready to start my trip from Caracas to crossing the Amazon jungle, to reach the area where members of this organization were supposedly already working.

Before leaving for my trip, one of my sisters showed me an aerial photograph from National Geography of the Amazon rainforest. A few hours later I was painting a phosphorescent white cross on the roof of the red truck, with the typical fantastic illusion –ignorant about it as I was –thinking that it might be easier for the air rescue team to find me, just in case I got lost for a long time.

Once again I was proving to myself that I was literally, as some people say, an asphalt flower. The idea of jungle that I had was what the movies *Tarzan*, *Gorillas in the Mist* and *Medicine Man* had created in my mind. My naivety sinned of ignorance, amid the fear of not having any way of communicating with anyone during the trip (there were no cell phones, no GPS and no short frequency radio).

Before leaving, I went to the house of the Hindu organization located in Caracas. No one was there at the time, but they had left an envelope on the door with my name, where there were several sheets of paper with the names of potential people who would be in Brazil, so that I could find them and drawings with possible routes to take.

Along the way, I made technical touches at the gas stations and took the opportunity to increase the number of copilots (ice for the cooler, bags of potato chips, sandwiches, soft drinks, maps of South America that I was finding, etc.).

The mechanics books were one of the most appreciated things, since in addition to being a human being made of asphalt, I did not know anything about mechanics.

From Caracas to the Brazilian border in southern Venezuela, there were about 1600 miles of totally or partially paved roads. The adventure until now was mainly focused on driving in heavy rain and little or no illumination on the roads, as well as sleeping in gas stations next to huge transnational cargo trucks.

From the beginning of the trip, the truckers were becoming my most reliable guides. Sharing with them I began to learn something about mechanics to how to carry out the necessary paperwork in the customs offices at the border. They gave me general advice for the road, as well as how to avoid police patrols, and many other important things that I could find on my way to the jungle.

Of course, every day I was more scared of what I was doing. Each truck driver took the opportunity to explain to me, in his own words or through horrible stories, all the risks I was taking and how crazy I was. From guerrillas to thieves, from local native Indians to corrupt military personnel, and a very heterogeneous and illustrated variety of potentially dangerous situations that I could face.

These stories, and the potential danger I was facing, were an extremely effective treatment for my temporary insanity. Bowel movements began to manifest my state of mind.

The Spaniards have a saying: "When they release the bull, either you run or you fight it." I really wanted to run!

Following the advice that the truckers gave me, I went to cross the border just at dawn, having the passport open and the papers from the truck ready to show them, as soon as the customs officer approached my window. It was perfect. He didn't ask any questions or check the truck, and in less than five minutes I crossed from Venezuela to Brazil and continued on to Boa Vista.

This was the first time I felt that what was happening to me was more than just luck or the direct result of truckers' advice. I felt that I was really accompanied by guardian angels. I use plural, because throughout this assignment, mission, adventure or madness, there were a lot of them, and I even think they took turns at trying to keep me mentally healthy and physically alive.

As soon as I crossed the border, the road changed – no more asphalt! Heavy rains and mud made the trip to Manaus long and difficult. Being stuck in the mud for hours, waiting for a military truck to pass by to help me, was the common denominator on this leg of the trip to Manaus.

Arriving in Manaus and observing the surprising difference in the color of the water between the Rio Negro and the Amazon rivers, which almost forms a perfect line at their confluence, was truly a unique experience. I parked my truck near the river, in a perfect position to enjoy both the magic of the moon reflecting its light on the water and the confluence of both rivers.

At midnight, a half-crazy thought of wild nature not only woke me up totally, but it filled me with an almost uncontrollable, adventurous spirit. And without further ado, I entered the river totally naked at the confluence level. The moon was so bright that I could see around me without any difficulty. After swimming for several minutes, experiencing the emotion of the direct contact with nature, I saw a man with a flashlight very close to my truck, signaling and yelling at me. I didn't understand what he was saying, but the body language was clear –

something imminent was happening, that deserved my immediate attention.

For those moments, my fears and reactions were the characteristics of someone who comes from a great metropolis, constantly managing multiple conflicting emotions. The first thing that came to my mind was that someone did something to the truck or something was stolen from me. I began to swim towards the man, whom I could not see clearly. As I got closer, his voice became clearer and clearer, the depth of the river decreased, and I began to walk fast, trying to raise my knees above the water. The man began to approach me, without going into the water. When the distance between us was reduced enough to detail our anatomies, I stayed on my knees, trying to hide that I was totally naked. The man shouted with more and more force in Portuguese. I tried to guess what he was saying by using my Spanish and what little I had learned by then in Portuguese.

I could guess, without much precision, that he was trying to tell me something about how dangerous it was to be naked in the water at night. The great thing is that I was more concerned about my nudity than what he was trying to warn me about. He repeated more or less the same thing several times, with increasing determination and with some mixed anguish. It did not take me long to understand his message: 'Be careful', with something about a thin and dangerous fish that can get through my anus.

At that moment, I proved to myself that I am a chicken, a first-class coward, and absolutely fearful of the animals of nature. Try to visualize a man running through the water, from a silent movie from the early 1900s – that's how I felt running, trying to jump over the water in an inordinate effort to get out of the river as fast as I could. Trust me, the last thing that came to mind was nudity.

The man was laughing for hours after I got out of the water. We stayed drinking *cachaça*, a very popular alcoholic beverage in Brazil, as strong – or stronger – than Mexican tequila. For me, at that time, it was the Brazilian tequila. We stayed drinking and trying to understand each other in a true *portuñol*, the perfect mix between Spanish and Portuguese, almost until dawn. The truth is that after the fourth or fifth shot of *cachaça*, I think neither he nor I were aware of which language we spoke. What was true is that we understood each other quite well.

I forgot to tell you that between shots of cachaça, we drank beers.

The main topic of the conversation was an endless amount of different stories where this type of fish was the main protagonist. This man was called Joao, and he was a trustworthy representative of Amazonian fisherman folklore.

It was a very short but intense friendship. I don't think, in my life, that I have drank so many beers per hour. According to Joao, friendship was only true if both parties shared enjoying each other while drinking. Joao used to say that if you are not under the influence of alcohol, you are controlling your thoughts, your emotions and your feelings all the time; otherwise it was impossible to meet the real person who was sharing with you.

By the way, in Brazil, beer is drunk very cold. It is served in a bottle with its own individual cooler. The beer has to be *estupidamente gelata* – that is, it has to be so cold that the beer is almost stupid.

Joao helped me find the way to cross the Amazon River. It took us five days to find someone who could cross me to a point where I could find a way into the jungle. During those five days I met many of Joao's friends, as well as several natural sons whom he introduced to me with a look and smile of pride.

For those five days the truck stayed parked among the fishermen's boats, and I slept in hammocks that hung between the boats, along with several of the fishermen. Joao went to sleep at his house. The fishermen invited me to eat at dawn and around six in the afternoon. The food was mainly fish, grilled over firewood on bonfires that they prepared between the boats, accompanied by white rice, yucca and feijoada, that the fishermen's families sent. This feijoada was a typical dish prepared with black beans and pieces of meat of different types.

My Portuguese really improved a lot, thanks to the intensive bar classes around the *estupidamente gelada* beers. Of course, in those five days, the main topic of each conversation was about how crazy I was to go alone into such an unpredictable, hostile jungle environment. Any person, woman or man and of any age, who passed in front of the little bar where we were, Joao asked them to sit with us, and of course, each of them gave his/her opinion about my trip, which, during those days, became more potential than real. Opinions that ranged from horrible crimes to lost forever in the middle of the jungle, filled the environment in the midst of a constant drinking spree. Thanks to the beers and *cachaças* I survived all those comments. Maybe drinking beers made my brain loke them... "estupidamente gelata"...

It was time to leave Manaus. By then there were already a lot of known people, who in a very unique and special way took care of me, while they adopted me emotionally and existentially. It was difficult and quite sad for me to leave them. At times, I thought and felt that my journey ended there, and that perhaps my mission was to stay with all those good people who were so special and so authentic.

We shared emotions, feelings, goals, dreams, and stories. Many ties were created between us. Many children and adolescents, who spent practically the whole day around me, engraved their looks and their smiles in my mind and in my heart. It was hard to leave them. We all knew it was a real goodbye. Many of them were already deep in my heart, and somehow I knew I was in theirs.

At the time of leaving, many of them accompanied me until the truck was mounted on a rather rustic iron barge. The barge was big enough to fit my pickup truck and a small cargo truck. In the cabin of the barge there was the room of the driver and his assistant, as well as a small kitchen with a table and two wooden benches.

Before leaving Manaus, my friends helped me equip the truck with things that were necessary, including four twenty-liter metal gasoline containers. My friends from Manaus did not allow me to pay for anything, not even food and drink. Every time I insisted on paying, they commented that when a friend comes to their house, it is to share and enjoy, and that everything is at the host's expense.

You can already have a clearer idea of how difficult it was to say our goodbyes.

Due to the currents of the Amazon River, it took us more than two days to reach the point, previously chosen, on the other side of the river. This point was south of the Rio Negro. During this trip on the barge, I was able to experience what the piranhas of the Amazon were all about. The driver stopped at a place on the south bank of the river to buy a cow. It was a very small local indigenous community that lived in primitive dwellings on the bank of the Amazon River. Somehow I was excited to see these natives and how they did business.

But this emotion quickly turned into a cruel scenario. The cow was alive. The natives pushed the cow into a large hole in the ground, where they beat her to death on the head. Then, with great effort, about six or seven people put her inside the barge towards the side of the captain's cabin. Due to the small free space in the barge, the cow's hind legs were under the loading truck.

The captain moved the barge forward a few hundred meters and then stopped. He asked me to help him. I wanted to do it to be supportive, but I really couldn't, so I tried to escape the commitment by telling him that I didn't have the guts to do it. Thank God he understood, and without rhyme or reason, he began to prepare everything to start skinning the cow.

I felt selfish, but the truth is that I was scared, and in a way I was worried about the mess this guy was going to make around my truck van and the cargo truck. When he started to cut it, the cow moved and hit the truck, breaking one of its headlights. I jumped in to help him. To be honest, I believe I did it to protect my truck. I don't want to go into details, but it really was a bloody mess. The blood, the smell, the flies, the prevailing disorder and the uncomfortable place distorted my thinking and my feeling, leaving them submerged in a limbo of horror for almost the whole two hours it took them to tear the cow to pieces. I think the dizziness, the nausea, and the repeated vomiting contributed to my mental state. The captain was laughing and joking all the time about my weakness in this regard. Even after I washed and cleaned myself, as an obsessive, compulsive, unbalanced being, the smell and images of that moment stayed with me for weeks.

Every time I stuck my head out of the barge to vomit, I saw the horrible sight of hundreds of piranhas eating what was left of the cow. Due to the frequent visits of different types of animals during the first days on my way through the Amazon rainforest, I think many residues of that cow were hidden under the truck.

After surviving trying to get the truck off the barge without it falling into the water, I stayed the rest of the day and night right where the captain left me. I was not feeling very well, physically or emotionally. I think the whole idea of the Amazon exploded inside me. They were hours of crying, insecurity, fear, and frightening mixed feelings. The cow episode wasn't really cruel, it was just new and different for me, but for everyone involved, it was part of their life or their survival needs.

I started to really feel what I was beginning to face, and that scared me. Praying in the form of speaking with an invisible and imaginary friend was my best support and copilot. This was the beginning of a long and daily talk with the angels who were with me throughout this missionary adventure.

The solitude, the astonishing beauty of the sunset, the deep darkness of the night, the fascinating magnificence of the stars, the concert of unique and, in many cases, terrifying noises, generated in me the feeling that this was the beginning of the end for me, without having a clue that I really was on the verge of the end of the beginning.

The weakness product of the conflicts between my thoughts and feelings, as well as physical fatigue, played an important role in helping me sleep most of the night.

The next morning, I woke up before dawn and set out to take what at the time seemed like the final steps of my life. The sunrise seen from the Amazon River really gave a touch of heaven to my disposition to continue. Actually, there was no well-marked road, nor a clear and uniform road. Jump after jump of the truck was what designed the menu for the first day. I just limited myself to following the compass towards the south and southeast.

By early afternoon I was already experiencing the tropical rain. Since that afternoon, and for a few days after, I couldn't see the sky anymore, only dense vegetation and the most amazing variety of flying and crawling insects. Just before dark, I decided to stop driving. There was no specific place to park the truck. I tried to park it in a way that left as much space as possible for another vehicle to pass, in case it appeared.

The long hours driving through such a difficult and rugged road, associated with the whirlwinds of conflicting emotions, left me so exhausted, and before dark I was already sleeping in the truck's cabin inside the sleeping bag. In the middle of the night, I woke up and thought I was dead. It was so dark that I couldn't even see my hands near my eyes. It was like being a soul without a body. Tapping around, I found a flashlight. This was a special, powerful flashlight that plugged into where the truck's cigarette lighter was. I started the engine and connected the plug, and a powerful light came on from the flashlight that illuminated the entire interior of the truck, which was great, mainly for finding the pillow, getting a Coke out of the cooler, and making myself a sandwich. While enjoying this dinner at midnight, I came up with the bright idea, or rather the naive idea, of pointing the light into the dense darkness outside the truck.

I find it difficult to find the words that can come close to describing, in detail, the amount of bright things that were reflected, and the new and different noises that were generated in crescendo. I don't think I remember another moment in my life as scary as those minutes were. As a reflex action, I turned off the flashlight and verified that the doors were properly closed. I covered myself completely with my sleeping bag and began to repeat like a mantra what originated from my gut: *coño, coño, coño, coño!* I fell asleep sitting on the floor between the pedals and the seat.

Note: only a Spanish-speaking person understands the true meaning of the expression: *coño, coño, coño, coño.* Just to try to give an approximation, it would be something between, Holy crap! Holy cow! Shit! Holy smoke! Fuck! Holy moley! but not said in a vulgar nature, manner or essence.

This word *coño* became an important component of my vocabulary for many weeks. It was used in different ways and for different circumstances, and in a magical way, it really helped me a lot, not only emotionally but also to survive my varied daily experiences.

By now, about fifteen days had passed since I left Caracas. On me was less weight and more smell and still having no idea what I was doing in the middle of that muddle riot mess. The first three days were quite similar: fear and surviving the road, the swamps, the constant rain, the black and super dark nights, as well as the emotions and feelings associated with a strange and very significant feeling of loneliness.

By the fourth day or so, I began to find vast areas devastated by deforestation —— a deforestation that felt immoral and malicious. Large areas among the jungle, where the destruction of trees was total, were like oases of desolation in the middle of the jungle. Despite being somewhat happy to see the sky again and to find my way more easily, I was really sad and disappointed to be witnessing the destructive selfishness of the human being to that dimension. The contrast was like seeing the flesh-eating bacteria devouring the surrounding skin.

By then I was crossing the equator line. The days and nights were different. Now, from time to time, I would meet some people, most of them garimpeiros. These were the former informal miners who came from low-income regions and without major economic opportunities, who gathered in groups and lived in houses built rustically on barges. They moved through the jungle with the idea of looking for gold, diamonds and other precious stones, but in reality they were traffickers of drugs, gold, tropical and exotic birds, and they helped people to enter the areas where they could cut trees, etc.

I shared with them on multiple occasions, mainly in the early hours of the night. Among alcoholic beverages of all kinds, they liked to tell their life stories and the difficulties they faced daily in their survival. I was with them as someone different from them, but at no time did I judge them. They were very nice people who, unfortunately, did not know any other way to survive. They respected me and asked me to wait somewhere when they were selling drugs or doing something illegal. They knew very well what was right and what was wrong. They had their own rules and their own laws. Many of them were Yanomami Indians who spoke Portuguese well.

The nights at the equator line gave me the most beautiful and extensive scenery of stars that I have ever seen. I could see stars beyond the Milky Way – at least that was what I thought and what they told me when I was sitting with the garimpeiros in their barges. Many of them seemed to have a fair amount of knowledge of the stars and constellations, which they shared with me and spent hours pointing out special constellations and stars to me in the sky. Unfortunately, I didn't quite understand what they were saying to me, since they mixed their dialects with Portuguese, but I understood the essence of the message.

One of the most horrible and disgusting events that I experienced was when they started hunting tropical birds, especially parrots, toucans, and macaws. They silently approached the area where they were stationed and then threw a homemade explosive. The shock waves from the explosion disturbed their flight, and they fell to the ground and into the water without being able to walk or fly for several seconds. Then a lot of these garimpeiros ran towards them, and others jumped into the water to catch them with fishing nets. Some of the birds recovered quite quickly and managed to escape; others more unfortunate died by drowning in the river. More were the birds that died than those that were caught.

They emotionally covered up their miserable actions by deluding themselves, saying that this was the jungle and that was the way to survive it. On this occasion, I could not hide my disappointment and could not contain myself expressing my judgment. They stared into my eyes and listened to my outrageous comments about it, and then we continued to share as if nothing had happened. I was left with the impression that they did not understand what I tried to convey to them.

In Manaus, they told me a lot about the garimpeiros and their way of life, but nothing compared to living it directly. It was not easy for me to continue as if nothing had happened, and several hours later, in the midst of a few drinks, I asked them about the military who was supposed to prevent the occurrence of this type of atrocities. They replied that they knew their itinerary very well, as well as those who patrolled the area. At times they had been caught, and what they asked for was some money. And with several "Benjamins," as they called the hundred-dollar bills, the military not only did not bother them, but sometimes made their work easier.

I kept moving south. For days I was again deep in the jungle where it rained a lot, and I couldn't see the sky. The roads were again very narrow and confusing to follow. This was mainly due to recent rains that caused rivers and streams in the area to overflow. Between the poor visibility, due to the fog and rain, and the unexpected potholes and holes in the road that hid under the mud, around noon on the third day, in this new part of the jungle, while I was driving, a large amount of smoke suddenly began to come out from the front of the pickup truck, accompanied by a strange noise. It paralyzed my heart in its tracks.

Thank God that my heart continued beating in the midst of the panic that invaded my mind, my emotions, my feelings, and a series of other things that I leave to the discretion of your imagination.

The first thing that came to mind was that the engine had burned out. I got out of the truck and went out to open the hood, with a strange uncertainty of wanting to know and at the same time not wanting to know what was happening. After opening it, even more white smoke was coming out of the engine. I went to the back of the pickup and took a large bottle of water out of the cabin and threw it on the engine, praying and asking God and all the angels that accompanied me that that that was the solution to the problem and not something serious.

The water decreased the amount of smoke, and I could see what was happening. Thank goodness it was a hole in the hose coming from the radiator. I instinctively acted as fast as I could, not as a mechanic but as a doctor. I took out a roll of white duct tape from the first aid box and began wrapping it around the hose hole. In the end, no more vaporized water came out of the engine. After finishing my surgical procedure, the hose seemed to have a white cast.

Not only that, but that cast lasted until I returned to Venezuela many months later.

As soon as I finished my first jungle surgery, I got back into the truck, and when I leaned back in the seat, an intense and almost unbearable pain, coming from different points of my back, shook me. In a reflex movement, I jumped out of the truck and took off the T-shirt I was wearing. There was a large variety of tiny, smelly bugs, from large black ones to gray and brown ones with horns. That T-shirt was my first gift that I gave to the Amazon rainforest. I left it there, with all the respective bugs mentioned.

By then, it had been approximately four to five weeks since I had left Venezuela. I was disconnecting myself from one of the determining variants of my life pattern – time. I had lost track of what day of the week it was. For several weeks, the counting of the Coca-Colas was the one that was giving me the time guidelines. I separated them by weeks, in a way that they could last until I got closer to civilization again. This was the reason why I knew that it had been around four to five weeks since my departure.

For the next two days, I couldn't go far. The rain and floods made driving very difficult. At the end of these two days, still raining but with less intensity, crossing a rudimentary bridge made of tree trunks, I had my first accident. The bridge broke, and the rear of the truck was left in the river, leaving the cabin and the engine out of the water, pointing upwards and supported by the front wheels that got caught between the trunks of the split trees. The broken logs held the truck so that it would not be carried away by the swollen river in the rain. The back of the pickup that was closed was flooded, and all that was in there was in a complete mess. Everything was floating in the water that was constantly entering.

In the passenger cabin, I was lying on the glass at the back, which allowed me to see into the rear cabin. All the things in the cabin had fallen on me. The creaking of the pickup bodywork, the noise of the water making turbulence in the rear part that was under the water, the noise produced by the river and its solid contents hitting the metal parts of the truck, put my heart, my mind and my soul in the preparatory steps for my takeoff to the other world.

In the first few hours, I was afraid to move, thinking that if I moved, the truck would finish descending towards the river. After praying for hours, without ever using the word *coño*, I fell asleep in the same position until the next morning.

Imagine how scared I was not to have said any bad word. The next morning it was no longer raining, the force and the amount of water in the river was decreasing little by little, and with the light of day I could see the disaster from the back of the truck. Everything there was mixed with mud and pieces of tree branches and leaves, in such a way that it was impossible to save anything.

I changed to a more comfortable position and made "my room" more appropriate for the occasion. I spent two days looking at the tall trees and the light between their branches. Roughly every hour during the day, I honked the pickup horn several times, and at night I turned on the light of the powerful flashlight that I mentioned earlier and pointed it outwards, moving it from side to side for a few minutes at a time. This I repeated approximately every twenty to thirty minutes until I fell asleep. They really were very long days and nights. By then, I was having regular and repetitive conversations out loud with my teammates and copilots. In the middle of the morning of the third day, a military convoy rescued me.

The truck survived without major damage, but everything in the rear cabin was destroyed. The tires and engine were undamaged. I followed the military convoy to their camp, where a mechanic checked the truck. I stayed with them for two days. Each of them had a complete physical examination. Some of them had skin diseases like leprosy, leishmaniasis, and scabies, without really caring about them. Everyone was eager to speak and share their own experiences in the Amazon region. They, unsurprisingly, were eager to hear about the Venezuelan women. They gave me an extraordinary map of the Amazon region, with all the smallest details.

I left the camp and drove south. After about ten to twelve hours of driving, I began to pass through huge estates (*fazendas* in Portuguese). I say huge, because crossing each one of them can take you from half a day to almost two days. There were estates with several small communities, like small towns, within them. I went through the vast majority of them. The people were simple and very nice. The children spent most of their time around the truck, jumping in and out of it. There was a kind of barter – I shared my skills as a doctor, and they shared their food with me. What we ate together was mainly black beans, rice, avocado and fruits from the area. I gave them general medical checkups to give them treatment and prevention advices, based on what they had around them. I really felt fabulous. A strange constant happiness began to invade my soul, my spirit and my mind. I was significantly more self-assured and less scared. Meeting new people while on this trip had become a true spiritual experience.

Within week seven or eight of my departure, I reached my first assigned mission. I arrived in the late afternoon, and there was no one around, but there was evidence that many people lived there. It even smelled like there was something cooking inside. The doors of the houses were open, but I stayed next to the truck, waiting. About an hour after sunset, I heard voices coming from a nearby forest in the distance. I moved the truck so that I could point the headlights at them.

There were about thirty people, most of them women of different ages and all of them dressed in orange robes. They were waiting for me, but they didn't know exactly when I was supposed to show up. A woman in her sixties was in charge of the group. They showed me where to park the truck and a space where I could sleep in my sleeping bag on the floor. After cleaning the truck a bit and taking my belongings to the room where I was supposed to stay, I went to have dinner with them. So far I did not know who these people were and why they were dressed in orange.

After sharing dinner with them, where everyone ate in silence, I managed to hear some things that some people were saying in low voices, and I learned that they went to the forest to meditate at the end of the afternoon until nightfall.

This reception left me in a state of shock, perhaps in a state of mental trance, where I did not know whether to cry or run from there.

At the end of dinner, in the midst of deathly silence, a group of about three to four people collected the dishes and took them to the back. I stood there, observing, without actually observing anything. I was half confused. I was not at all familiar with situations or people like these.

After an hour or two of dinner, the woman in charge, named Ananda, began to explain to me about them and what I could do while I was with them. This community was in the mountains outside the state of Sao Pablo. There were three houses. One was quite large, where the kitchen, the dining room and the three bedrooms for the women were located. The other house was approximately one hundred square meters, where the classrooms for the education of the members of the surrounding communities were located, and the third was a house of approximately sixty square meters, still under construction. There was a shower outside the big house and a toilet in a small 1.5 by 1.5-meter-square space outside, approximately thirty meters from the big house. There was only one door in front of the main house. The rest of the house used thin fabric curtains to divide the rooms and as doors.

I stayed in the little house under construction. It was a cement brick house with a large interior space and no partitions. The holes for three windows and a door were already made, and only the door had a plastic curtain. I positioned myself in the corner of the back of the house. Some seven to eight boys slept intermittently in that house. They slept on the floor on handmade straw rugs.

All of them were part of a congregation based in northern India and Nepal, called "Ananda Marga," that was dedicated to building small communities around the world, where nature was incorporated as an integral part of their lives. They were vegetarians, they ate what they could grow, and they were incorporated into the life cycle of the environment around them, in such a way that no living creature was harmed or disturbed. They meditated three times a day. The first time was from an hour before sunrise to an hour later, then from an hour before sunset to an hour after, and then an hour after dinner over a two-hour period.

They trained in meditation following the teachings of Sathia Sai Baba and Prabhat Ranjan Sarkar (Shrii Shrii Ánandamúrti). The organization had three master gurus who spent most of the time meditating in the mountains of Nepal. Twice a year, one of them visited communities around the world. They all had a Sanskrit name. During the day, they worked on the crops around the houses, all wearing brown, coarse, cloth robes. For meditation and to sleep, they wore orange robes.

After talking with Ananda for more than two hours, and without being able to talk to anyone else, I went to my corner and got into the sleeping bag, facing the wall. I was still in shock. I slept with two chocolates hidden inside the sleeping bag, since I could not eat but a few bites – the vegetarian dishes at dinner were not very appetizing for me.

Despite my hunger, the state of shock I was in did not allow me to swallow well.

Try to imagine the countless mixed thoughts and feelings that crossed my mind during all those hours, jumping back and forth from my heart to my brain and vice versa. I was so confused that I was not able to distinguish between my stupidity and my naivety. This was not a fall into reality, this was a thrust that carried the same intention as that of the bullfighter in a bullfight.

At that time I was a Catholic person, in the traditional way. I had never been involved with Hinduism, meditation, the vegetarian lifestyle, or those kinds of hippie-happy-naturist-surreal communities. In the midst of my uncertainty, I did not know how to accept reaping the fruits of what I had been sowing. My ego insisted on constantly sending messages to my mind to seek responsibility in others, and my thoughts were focused on repeatedly asking myself the question: Why, in the name of fairness and justice, did no one tell me anything about this? I thought that I was supposed to work for a Catholic mission, or at least a Christian or a Jewish one, that I at least knew a little about, but to work for people who based their life on Hinduism, naturism and an existence... for me, in those moments, it was surreal. It wasn't on my agenda.

In those hours, inside my sleeping bag, I learned that the first thing I had to do was get rid of my agenda and open my mind and my heart to what was not written in my agenda. I became aware of my existential, spiritual, and religious insecurity. What it was up to at that moment was only a preamble to what I was potentially beginning to discover about my destiny. I was much more immature than I thought. I had deluded myself into thinking that with my mind trained in logistics and neurology, there was room to understand and accept a type of missionary work like this.

Between the frustration, the nervousness, the confusion and the madness, suddenly I started to laugh just thinking of God's sense of humor. Maybe I was freaking out already, but I really felt better and was able to sleep until before dawn, when everyone in my room started to go out for their morning meditation session.

I stayed a while longer, between being asleep and awake, semi-sitting and leaning against the wall until one of the terrestrial creatures created by God approached me. It seemed that it was trying to kiss me or get in the sack with me. It was still so dark, and I was half confused from waking up in a strange place, so my brain was not yet registering what was happening. I pushed the creature – not really knowing what it was –instinctively. Between the dream and the reverie, I thought that one of the boys had returned and I was tripping over his foot.

But, unfortunately and unexpectedly, I was very wrong. It was a live armadillo, which, of course, I did not immediately identify. This thing was warm and hard, and it came back every time I pushed it. This back and forth relationship between it and me was what made my brain start working in different potential directions. Due to the inevitable emotions of fear and unpleasant sensations after the last push, I directed my hand towards a flashlight. When I turned it on, I immediately changed my position, where I went from semi-sitting to standing in a second, followed by the subsequent race out of the house, not knowing what to do or where to go. When I calmed down, I returned to the house and pointed the flashlight at the creature until it walked out, which was when I could identify it.

I went to the truck and sat inside for a while. I realized that the boys had got up earlier than I thought, since there were no movements in the big house, and it was still very dark. I fell asleep and woke up to the noise of the women in the big house. I waited a few moments for everyone to go out into the forest to meditate and took the opportunity to bathe in the only shower there was. Of course, it was an effective shower, but quick, since it was cold water that fell without pressure, in addition to being before six in the morning, since it had not yet dawned. As soon as I got dressed, I went to inspect the complex before they returned. Everything smelled of a rather strange mixture of different types of incense. On the floor of each room were photographs of different Nepalese and Hindu gurus, and in front of them were several burning incense sticks. There were no chairs or tables. Everything from eating to sleeping was done on the floor. The only place higher than the floor was a long concrete table in the kitchen where the kerosene cooking device, kitchen utensils, fruits and vegetables were located. The toilet was a hole in the ground, which meant that every few days the toilet was moved to a new and different location around the main house. All the natural waste was placed inside a large hole in the ground, which was approximately eight to ten meters from the kitchen.

After each meal, whatever was left over was thrown into the hole and covered with banana leaves and soil. It was a compost heap of about three-by-three meters. From there they took out compost to fertilize the crops. Maybe it sounds very nice and with a great natural spirit and protection of the environment, but from a practical point of view, due to imperfections in the processes involved in composting, it seemed a rather important lack of hygiene, at least for me.

I say this, since this compost was very close to the kitchen and the smells were very strong and unpleasant, all the surroundings with food waste in various periods of decomposition, in addition to the hundreds of hundreds of flies that were kept in and around this "composting" with so much freedom, it gave the impression that for them it was their earthly paradise.

The first day, I began to walk around alone, since everyone else was so busy working on their respective assignments, that just a "hello" was the only communication I could have from them, when I was passing by. There were so many young adolescents –no older than twenty or twenty-one years old – working and acting as hypnotized slaves, that it generated a strange sensation of social and family maladjustment.

They believed with such conviction that self-inflicted mortification and hard work helped them attain a higher level of spirituality, that I did not try to tell them anything that went against what they were living in that place. During their meditations, which I attended more as an observer than as an active participant, I could appreciate that apparently a disconnection with the world existed in them, some because they seemed to be in contact with their inner silence, and a great majority because they fell asleep.

After several days, Ananda, the leader of the complex, told me that that night it would be a ceremony to officially introduce me to the whole group, and where the corresponding rituals would be performed to join the organization. So it was, that after dinner, everyone met in one of the rooms, all sitting cross-legged in a lotus position, except for me, who was sitting in a bizarre position, due to the muscle cramps the lotus position gave me in the legs every time I tried to cross them like they did. In front of me, the three leading women were seated in an almost perfect lotus position and, behind them, the rest of the thirty-something members. For about ten to fifteen minutes, they all sang very intoned and beautiful songs, which unfortunately I did not understand. At the end of the chant, everyone leaned forward, touching their foreheads to the ground, as a welcome greeting to me. Then the ceremony began. The three leading women closed their eyes and remained silent, without being interrupted by anything. I could hear the sound of many people's breaths, but not theirs.

After almost an hour of silence, where everyone had their eyes closed except me, Ananda said something in Sanskrit. She asked me to face her and sit cross-legged, in the lotus position, with my back straight. She took in her hands a bunch of big cards with pictures of animals on them. They all started singing again together, and after a few minutes she said a very loud Sanskrit word. They all stopped singing and stared at me. A few seconds later, she threw the cards into the air in front of me, moved them with her fingertips and took one of her own. It was a card with the image of an otter. She grabbed it between her fingers and showed it to everyone present. They all laughed and started clapping. I felt honored, but my natural shyness for these things took control of my emotions and feelings. In the face of all this, no matter how hard I tried, and the more effort I made, I still felt like a cockroach in a hen dance. (Venezuela saying: meaning to feel totally out of place.)

Apparently, the otter was an animal similar to me or something like that, from what I understood. Later, she gave me my name with which I would identify myself in the congregation; the name was in Sanskrit. Really, I could never learn it. I had it written down on a piece of paper that I kept in my pocket, and I consulted it several times a day. What I do remember is that it meant "ascending light." I never asked how or why they chose that name. I could only recognize its sound to respond when someone called me.

I think it is important that I tell you that since you have embarked on the adventure of reading this book, that I am dyslexic – what is known as developmental dyslexia (a disorder characterized by difficulties in learning to read and in processing of certain sounds). In addition, I have selective memory difficulties for names (dysnomia) and remembering numbers, as a result of a head injury with a skull fracture that I had at the age of five years old.

The first weeks were very difficult for me. I tried to adapt to the place and to the day-to-day activities. I received introductory disciplines for the daily meditation sessions. The hardest part was trying to avoid muscle cramps in my legs and back while in the meditation position that they directed me to do. I had an assigned and apparently personal mantra. The vegetarian diet and the quality of the food fervently took care of me taking weight off my body as the days went by. On many occasions, feelings of guilt invaded my mind. My strong Catholic background was in a daily battle against my new daily meditation practices and identification with a very selective Hindu congregation. In many ways I was part of them. I lived in their community, practiced their religious disciplines, wore the same kinds of clothes, and they saw me with them all the time.

After having been getting to know the environment for a couple of weeks, I presented to Ananda a project oriented to creation of small units of preventive and curative medicine based on the incorporation of what was known about the natural cycle life of local communities. To avoid the natural reflex reaction of rejecting innovations, the presentation of the presented project emphasized the benefits it would bring to the leaders, and directly to the Hindu congregation. After discussing with the rest of the community and with the leaders of the organization in South America, the project began a few days after its presentation.

During those days of waiting, I was driving to explore the surroundings, within a radius of about three hundred kilometers from where we were. I was able to visit a wide variety of small villages and isolated communities. In addition to getting to know its inhabitants, there was an opportunity to talk to them about the potential benefits of the project. In a surprising way, almost all the people I met were very receptive and enthusiastic to help and participate in the project, to the limit of their possibilities. The four days that I spent touring all these places were really inspiring for me. I felt like I was in the right place and doing what I was supposed to do.

Once the project was approved, we began to visit schools, city halls, municipalities and churches in the surroundings, to present the project to them and to design the logistics with them. Three people from the Hindu community were with me the whole time: two women leaders, and a boy named Damesio, twenty years old and who had been with the congregation for more than six years. Damesio was a natural artist. He could paint murals from his mind, as if he were writing a letter. One of the leaders played the guitar and sang beautifully with an angelic voice that transported you to magical places.

As we received the go-ahead from the local Portuguese authorities, we began to create groups in the different centers that offered their help. Each group was made up of local people. Subgroups were created with different tasks, including subgroups of builders, kitchen helpers, singing and teaching first aid. Two hours of talks were given to each community, usually in a local church. Conversations with people started very early in the morning, and during the day, until late at night, mainly in the communities where most of the people were working late. Ninety to ninety-five percent of the talks were based on medical-care topics.

People asked all kinds of questions related to their own medical problems. In each talk there was a person who helped improve communication in both directions. This was mainly due to my strange mix of Caribbean Spanish, uneducated Portuguese, and English. The mixing of English in my new daily vocabulary was the result of sharing with people in the Hindu congregation, where many different ways of speaking the English language flourished in everyday communication.

In a few days, the physical spaces for the project were arranged and painted by the construction group and artistically decorated by Damesio. Before and after the talks, the lead woman, Yiya, played the guitar and sang with everyone. She spoke Portuguese perfectly. Her name came from ying and yang. It was an extraordinary experience. We were all so happy and satisfied with what we were doing, that on many occasions we went all day without eating. In general, we ate fruits and avocados, while driving from one place to another. Avocados in Brazil were eaten as a fruit, the same as mango, orange or apple. We were the only ones in the congregation who did not participate in the daily meditation sessions.

This played a huge role in my happiness back then. Inside the truck, the two women were sitting in the front with me and Damesio in the back. During the trips from one place to another, the three of them would meditate, which made me the only heathen on the team.

The local churches and organizations of Christians, evangelists and Catholics were the local people most involved in the project. We had been teaching first-aid medicine using local remedies, natural elements and dietary information, including instructions on how to learn to use the power of thought without interfering with the balance of the environment. In some places, we met every two or three days with groups of alcoholics, drug addicts and people infected with the HIV virus or with AIDS, creating a kind of group therapy. Each local church or religious group was responsible for meeting them in one place, three times a week.

During the first months, there were no differences between a Monday and a Saturday. We used to leave the Hindu congregation every morning at the same time as the rest of the people who began to walk into the forest for their meditation, and we usually worked until around midnight. None of us ever complained of being tired. We used to carry fruits and vegetables with us every day. After my coworkers finished their morning meditations, we ate breakfast in the truck while I was driving. What I was eating were mainly oranges and tangerines. I was not very fond of the other fruits or vegetables they carried. The truth is that I was not a friend of tomatoes, cucumbers, raw onions, etc.

Anyone in the western world knows that there is nothing better than a very hot cup of coffee in the morning, and more so at four a.m. before starting to drive your car, in a foggy mountain setting, in the early hours of the day. You cannot imagine how much my imagination had to work every morning, to produce the sensation in the body and in the mind, of the aroma, the taste and the warm sensations that a simple cup of coffee in the morning is capable of generating.

The type of Hindu congregation in which I was living was not only characterized by not eating animal meat, but also by not drinking beverages such as coffee, soft drinks, liquors, beers, etc. Thank God that when we arrived in the communities and small towns, the people there, who already knew me well, would wait for me with coffee, soft drinks or beers. To avoid any conflict, or hurt someone's feelings, they had them hidden, and as if we were little children, we went to a place where the rest of the team could not see me, and there we drank it, amid laughter and jokes. They said that if a coffee, a soft drink or a beer is not taken in the company of others, they lose all their essence and magic.

It was fascinating what this generated. It was an emotion of joy and contagious devilry that involved many local people; it was a fun conspiracy for all of us who participated in it. Those moments were very productive to build trust and friendship with the locals. In other places, they looked for me to rush to any house in the vicinity to eat a piece of meat or a plate of their food. I really enjoyed those moments immensely, plus they kept me fed, healthy, and alive. But most important of all, it allowed me to bring out my personality and my character, always mixed with humor, a spirit of adventure, secrets, and unpredictable things.

I had a hidden place in the truck, and these people filled it with food, chocolates, cookies, soft drinks, beers, and sometimes a bottle of local liquor. As you can see, my meditation moment was done alone in the forest, and it was quite different and quite unique – in other words, quite similar to me.

The days passed like flashes of lights, and time slipped by without feeling it. The satisfaction of a job done with efficiency and joy, the emotions and the results of it, as well as the intense daily schedule that it entailed, made my life during those weeks very special. In my heart grew the feeling of pleasure to help people just for the pleasure of doing it. Helping someone before circumstances put them in a position to ask for help is one of the most satisfying experiences any human being can have. The looks and facial expressions when someone in need of help receives it without asking for it are unique. It is like love, extremely difficult to describe, but extremely easy to experience. Every moment shared with those people, every facial expression, every look, every laugh, every tear that fell from their eyes was, for me, religion, church, happiness, love and the joy of experiencing God in those days.

Unfortunately, but not unexpectedly, the mysteries of humanity's unique condition began to emerge. Fears, jealousy and envy were mixed in different local groups of people, all of them with the truth in their hands. All this, together with the local political, social and religious pressure, began to generate exponentially a volcano of conflicting emotions.

One Saturday morning, the local police were waiting for us in the seven centers that were already open. The venues were closed, and we were asked to stay away from the communities.

We waited a few days to see if after the lava from the volcano cooled, there was the possibility of restarting what we were doing, but doing what the enemies wanted, in their own ways and with their own rules. Frustration, abuse of authority, arrogance and negativity were the only responses we got. A few days after the incident, the congregation leader received a telegram from her superiors, asking her to abandon this project and return to the routine they had before my arrival.

Unbeknownst to me at the time, this was the beginning of the end of my stay with the congregation. At noon on the day they received the telegram, they asked me to leave the congregation premises.

With acceptance and surprise, without saying a word, I put my belongings in the truck, leaving those that I had lent to the people of the congregation, and when they were walking to the forest in the afternoon to meditate, I left the premises. As I drove away, a strange sadness and uncertainty flooded me. There was not a goodbye or a word of solidarity for the time and shared work. I drove to the small town of Tatuí, where I spent the night with a local family who were my best friends in that part of the world. They were an exemplary family with a nobility and human quality that far exceeded normality. Since a few months ago, they made me feel like one of their family, in every moment we shared. They were also somewhat involved with the project. (Tatuí was the city where Ayton Senna, the famous Brazilian Formula 1 driver, had his farm with his own racetrack.)

Without questions, without hints, and without saying many words, my friends understood in their minds and hearts that I was going through a difficult time. The same night that I got to their home, they invited their relatives and neighbors, and they prepared some meats on a stake in the Brazilian style, accompanied by the famous, very special beers –*estupidamente geladas*. I stayed with them for a couple of days, thinking about what the next step in my life would be.

Still at my friends' house, someone from the Hindu congregation telephoned to deliver the message that one of the main leaders of the congregation, from Nepal, had come to the congregation compound and wanted to meet me. Without thinking for a minute, I left Tatuí, driving towards the house of the congregation. It took me almost five hours to get there. In the middle of the afternoon, I arrived in the community in the mountains and met the guru leader. He was a man of short stature, in his seventies, with a very slim build and weighing no more than forty-eight kilos. He was approximately 1,53 meters tall. He was dressed in an orange silk robe that covered his head and body, down to his feet. He was barefoot. I sat with him in a corner of one of the rooms used for group meditation. All kinds of burning incense sticks surrounded us. He had a special and kind facial expression. His skin was like a soft, copper pearl. He had a gentle, low-pitched voice. He spoke few words, mainly about me and my wildlife, as he called it. He told me a little about the universe that he felt and saw while he meditated. He mentioned that we were part of the whole universe in the same way that the universe was part of us. He was telling me that we are both connected beyond our human comprehension. He explained to me how meditation was a two-way opening with the universe. He told me that the universe constantly changed its forms and organization to the rhythm of the changes of consciousness of all its components, like when one sees through a kaleidoscope. Each of us has the freedom to move our assigned kaleidoscope at our own desire and risk. Life is just a human consciousness of our eternal existence.

Mastering meditation skills moves our universal self through different dimensions, in the perception of the magnificence of love. Any lifestyle is unique and great in its own special relationship with the universe.

Unfortunately, our fascinating conversation was interrupted by one of the local leaders. They told me that it was time for the master to begin his transmutation process. Grateful for the shared moment and the teachings received in such a short period of time, we said goodbye, saying "Namaste" as we flexed in front of each other, with our hands extended and close together at the height of the heart.

In the midst of this, the leaders asked me again to leave the premises, and walking towards the truck with one of the leaders, I asked her what that transmutation was. She quickly replied that it was a mysterious secret. She said goodbye to me several meters before reaching the truck. Driving slowly out of the place, I found the group of guys who were returning from their work in the crops. We stayed talking for a few minutes, and I asked them what the guru's transmutation process was about. From what I understood, the Guru Master had to immerse himself into a deep level of meditation until he entered in a special and unique trance with the evil part of the universe. The cosmic and astronomical conditions in that part of Brazil and during those two nights were somehow special for him to have that experience. It was one of the sacred secrets of the congregation. Each one of the members of the congregation, near sunset and singing special songs, would accompany him to the edge of the forest, where the guru would remain inside, totally alone, until the next dawn.

In my purposeful curiosity, I tried to ask if I could see it. I was interrupted just as my facial expressions began to change to express my intention. The interruption was a resounding "no," expressed in chorus. Immediately everyone started talking at the same time, saying that no one could see it, as there would be energies around that could kill or destroy the mind. With that, they told me to get out of the place quickly.

Without any intention of disrespecting anyone or committing any kind of blasphemy, I pretended to leave the area. I parked my truck in a hidden place from the congregation premises, about three to four kilometers from there. And scared to the bone, I started to run into the forest before dark, taking two flashlights with me. Thousands of feelings and thoughts of guilt, associated with a strange sense of warning, constantly invaded me as I walked into the forest. But, more than my human and neurological curiosity, it was a strange need to know what was going to happen inside the forest and what this fascinating man I had just met was going to do there.

In a strange way, my mind began to use reasons and justifications, but my heart tried to tell me that everything the guru told me was not by chance but that, between the lines, he was giving me the opportunity to take the initiative of exploring and question the contents of their words. I never really knew the whys of having been doing what I was doing, nor was I interested in them. I just wanted to see the guru in the forest. In the timeshare, although short for my wishes, I felt peace, intelligence, and divinity. And I was left with a strange desire to see him again, even for a few seconds.

As I came in from the opposite side of the forest, it took me more than two hours to approach the area where the master guru was already meditating. Thank goodness it was still clear enough to find my way. The full moon was my best help. I hid behind some old trees with very wide trunks. I sat for more than half an hour, leaning against one of the trees until my breathing calmed. Every ten to fifteen minutes I would come out of my hiding place and see the guru meditating in the distance. I got to this place around seven or eight p.m. I was very afraid that someone would discover me.

Multiple and varied noises that came from the forest were taking more and more prominence in my feelings of fear. It really was a long waiting period. Most likely, I had slept multiple times for several minutes at a time. After about two hours, I moved to another place where I could see him better and in front of me. I was lying between some trees about ten or twelve meters from him. The moonlight was reflecting on him, allowing me to see him quite well. He was meditating in the lotus position, with his back straight without the robe. He was in a dark-colored-surface forest clearing among several bushes. Suddenly and after more than three hours without having made any kind of physical movement, the guru began to move without altering his lotus position. I lay with my face against the ground, while my heart tried to leak out of my mouth. The only thoughts that crossed my mind were, *I am a dead man, I am a dead man.*

For about five to ten minutes, I just kept trying to control my breathing, without moving an inch of my body and with my gaze fixed on the guru. After my heart returned to my chest and my breathing became more regular, I lifted my face off the ground and saw the guru completely naked in the same meditation position as before. His body reflected the moonlight with a golden glow. I stared at him, and after an hour or so, the guru took several deep, loud breaths. Then he remained as if he was not breathing at all – at least, according to my observation ten or twelve meters from him. Then I thought I saw his body move. I got closer to him to get a better look at him and verified that he was actually moving. At first, there was a slow movement from side to side. It was so smooth that I thought he was floating in the air. For ten to fifteen minutes I was almost petrified looking at him. Strange feelings of nervousness and anxiety came over me. I was trying to stay calm without looking away from him. The slow movement from side to side almost stopped, at least in my perception. Then the most amazing thing began to happen – the guru began to levitate. Yes, I said levitate. This was not easy for me to assimilate at the time, nor was it easy for several years later. It took me many years to put it into words and communicate it to selected third parties.

The guru was about a meter from the ground, and his body was moving very slowly, rotating clockwise in circles. The terrifying feeling I was experiencing inside made me cry without being able to stop myself from doing so. I tried as much as possible not to make any kind of noise. After about half an hour, his body began to descend very slowly to the ground. He continued in his meditation position until dawn. Without the sun having risen yet, he stood up. He dressed in his orange robe and began to walk out of the forest in the direction of the congregation compound. As soon as he left the place, I went to check the area where he had been meditating. Nothing out of the ordinary. I even set my compass to check if there was some kind of magnetic field. But the compass, after many attempts, did not show any strange changes. I stayed for almost an hour, checking the area, and then I started running through the woods to my truck. I arrived in less than an hour. I drove to a service station about two hours from where I was, without being able to stop crying. I didn't know exactly why I was crying, but I couldn't control it. I parked the truck between some large cargo trucks, and I fell asleep. It was already dark when I woke up, and I was extremely hungry.

Since that night, and for many years after, there was not a moment in my life that I didn't think about what I saw in the forest. It became my own secret; not because it was very difficult for someone to believe what I had witnessed, or not, but because there was a strange blocking barrier that did not allow me to put into words what I saw.

For days I was in a kind of limbo. People around me thought I was depressed, but inside I knew that it was not an episode of depression.

As soon as I arrived in Tatuí, my friends began to use their influences to try to find a place where I could continue my idea of helping the most vulnerable people. My friends found out about a missionary group near the Iguazu Falls to the Brazilian side. I made the decision to go there. My departure from Tatuí was difficult and very emotional. I left part of my heart and part of myself there with my friends. We both knew that it would most likely be a forever goodbye in this earthly life experience. But for our divine essences, we knew it was just a "see you later."

I could not control my emotions and my feelings, and an intense sadness invaded me. It was so difficult for me to deal with all these new feelings that I couldn't drive for more than an hour at a time. I had to stop at almost every gas station that I came across along the road to rest or take a nap. There was no question – I was quite depressed and emotionally drained. My strength had almost run out. My energy level was at the lowest point I could remember, since I left Caracas. I was able to sleep from dusk to dawn the next day without waking up once.

It took me three days to get to the Iguazu Falls. The people that I was supposed to find there had left the place towards Paraguay. I waited for them for almost a week. During this time, I came across a group of Christian missionaries who were teaching the Bible readings. I accompanied them for five days through different communities on the Argentine side of the Iguazu region. These communities were formed mainly by local indigenous tribes. These indigenous tribes had adapted very well to capitalism. They wore normal clothes and were already involved in the brainwashing of capitalism. Their indigenous cultures and traditions were almost dissipated amid the mixture of superficial and materialistic needs and goals. While this group was teaching the Bible to the locals, I was doing physical exams and visiting the sick in their humble and rudimentary dwellings. It was very nice to reexperience my abilities to communicate my thoughts, feelings, and medical experience. Everyone there spoke Spanish. From the first day, this Christian group of about sixty men and women were already in full campaign to recruit me. This allowed me to have very interesting conversations with the vast majority of them.

It was a fascinating experience. They were five days of joy, enthusiasm, teamwork, and spirituality. In two days I was back to being the me that I liked to be. Unfortunately, on the fifth day they forced me to make a decision whether or not to join their church, and in less than an hour after they learned that this was not my main intention, in a very pleasant way they let me know that I could not continue with them. The diversity of spiritual ideas and freedom of belief were not on the agenda of this group. The only truth was theirs and had to be plunged into without questions.

I returned to the place where I was supposed to meet the missionary group on the Brazilian side of Iguazu, but there was no one there, and there was no message for me. I decided to spend a couple of days camping at the Iguazu Falls, mainly waiting for a new sign. After two days of local touring like a poor student, I decided to go to Paraguay to see what could happen there. In a week I crossed the country, driving through military checkpoints almost twice a day. I was nothing more than an absolute stranger, besides not having had the luck or the opportunity to find a way to help, and despite having visited dozens of churches, religious groups, and city halls. I left Paraguay and returned to Brazil.

I went to the city of Curitiba – a fascinating ecological city. The very first night of my arrival, I met a group of young artists who were there at an art festival. I stayed with them for a few days. It was a rather strange but didactic experience. There were about thirty of them, mainly from Uruguay and Argentina. The philosophical talks where the imagination played an important role were the best part of the daily conversations. Between the artistic ideas and dreams regarding the world and the influence of all kinds of legal and illegal psychostimulants of this group, at many times I would get lost in conversations, remaining like a little bird on golf a course – that is, watching from side to side to see where the ball was coming from. These people literally lived from day to day. They enjoyed what life had to offer them each day and didn't really care too much about what life held for them the next day. They thought that their simplicity made them experience happiness throughout life's journey.

With them I learned a bit about Uruguay and Argentina, as well as receiving a crash course on illicit street drugs and the potential dangers of being alone in those places. During those days I met a family of three – grandfather, father and son – who lived in Punta del Este, Uruguay. After two hours of talking about trivial things, the grandfather – named Antonio, if I remember correctly – propound me for the possibility of paying for gas, the motel and food, if I took them to Punta del Este in Uruguay, which was about seven hundred kilometers away. "Why not?" was my reflex response. It was a big change sleeping in a bed, taking long, hot showers, watching TV, eating good food at clean tables, and most important of all, sharing the journey with a very nice family of three generations.

The son stayed in the back of the truck, and the grandfather and father accompanied me in the cabin. I became familiar with the jokes and the idiosyncrasies of the Uruguayan. I almost became addicted to mate – a Uruguayan drink. It was fascinating how we shared the mate, drinking from the same metal straw. A cup of mate was prepared at the same time that it was shared, one sip at a time, and it was rotated. It took us three days and two nights to arrive. The rain, floods and fog made the journey longer.

After arriving in Punta del Este, I stayed for one day at this family's house. I was introduced to the relatives of one of the survivors of the plane crash of the rugby team in the Andes mountain range in the 1960s. In the house of the father of one of the survivors, there was a museum with all the details about the rescue operation and survival adventures in the frozen mountains of the Andes. One of these relatives arranged for me to meet with a congregation of the order of San Francisco, in Montevideo.

The next day I left early, driving to the Franciscan convent located on the outskirts of Montevideo. It was a 19th-century construction. For the first time I felt, in the spirituality of the Franciscan missionaries, what I imagined in my mind that I was going to experience before leaving Venezuela for this missionary adventure. It was a big and very cold place with few people around, mainly old Franciscan priests. I spent less than a week with them, mainly as a tourist. They didn't know what to do with me, and I couldn't figure out what to do around those places, either. One of the priests gave me a list of all the Catholic missionary places and groups in South America. He also gave me some information about other religious groups.

I left the convent one Saturday morning for Buenos Aires. I managed to find a service station on the outskirts of Buenos Aires, where they allowed me to park the truck and sleep there as long as I wanted. The place was very safe, and all the people around were very friendly. I was moving around on the local buses. I became friends with the owner of the service station, and his family. On several occasions, they invited me to dine with them. This family, upon learning that I was a neurologist, became true promoters and began to offer my professional services to the entire region for free. For two weeks I shared with different types of people from different socio-economic conditions. I saw patients in their homes, mostly with undiagnosed neurological problems or difficult medical problems. "Nothing better than having a doctor for free," was the motto they used. Some days, we literally hopped from house to house, from early in the morning until late at night. I was always accompanied by a member of this family. The father and one of the sons were the ones who accompanied me the most, and they felt "super good." They said that they felt like a candidate for a mayor doing a political campaign.

Every time we went to see someone, that someone, or his/her relatives, had someone else who wanted me to see them. I was happy, and they were happy. We were the perfect team.

I ate all kinds of local food, mostly desserts. There was no home that did not offer us something to eat or drink. I went to see people who were surrounded by candles and all kinds of witchcraft paraphernalia, as well as people where the family was sitting and praying. It was a great human and medical experience. I visited and prayed in so many different churches, most of them Catholic.

Buenos Aires was a true experience of friendship, with more than two weeks of giving and receiving in a harmonious and satisfactory way for both parties. I could say, without fear of being wrong, that we witnessed the experience of coherence, and perhaps also the one of synchronism. It was amazing to see how much help a doctor could give a family in distress. As a doctor, when I visit patients in their homes, I instantly become a priest, a sorcerer, a guru, a healer, and a friend. When a doctor went to their homes with no intention other than trying to help, it opened the doors for them to find their own healing for themselves.

Human contact in the home of the needy, between the doctor, the patient and his entire family environment, generated the forces of love, of compassion, of commitment and of solidarity that determined the guidelines of the art of practicing medicine.

This generation of energies taught those involved that the art of medicine did not lie in curing or trying to heal, but in showing solidarity with the pain and uncertainty of the patient and of his loved ones. The healing energy was generated from the patient's own divinity and from the divinities of loved ones that were shared with a common goal. Giving them a clinical diagnosis, determining a therapeutic alternative and organizing with the patient and their environment the ways to administer it, were the only means to calm the mind, while the heart sought a way to manifest its love in the form of a healing divinity.

At times, I felt that it was not me who visited the patient's home, but other divine entities who used me as a means to reach them. Finding the right words to say to a certain person, in certain circumstances, was not the result of my congenital or acquired abilities, but the result of an atmosphere of love that surrounded the environment. Sometimes I felt that there were so many invisible entities around, trying to help the patient and his/her family in any way possible, that I was just a simple observer.

The time had come to move on. Of course, it was difficult to leave behind the emotional ties experienced. But instead of tears, this time there were smiles of satisfaction. I left the surroundings of Buenos Aires and headed towards the southeast of Argentina to cross the famous countryside known as "Las Pampas," in the direction of San Carlos de Bariloche.

Rain, cold and light snow made the journey long, cold, and difficult. For a few days I was mainly driving, eating and sleeping. I was no longer the guy who could drive hours and hours without stopping. Drowsiness and exhaustion were already creeping up on me. My resistance was affected by the repercussions and connotations of my recent experiences. All of this was slowly sapping my daily strength and my action time, mercilessly and without even asking for permission.

Honestly, the image of the "Pampas" that I had in my mind and in my heart, as a result of so many stories, songs and movies, was significantly better than the one I was living driving through them. I had the opportunity to get to know, albeit superficially and ephemerally, some beautiful places of the fascinating city of San Carlos de Bariloche. With a local temperature of minus two to minus four degrees Celsius, most of the time I spent walking and eating, mainly the delicious chocolate of the region. I spent two nights sleeping in the truck, parked in different places. It was fascinating to see how the humidity of my breath froze inside the cabin at night, and I, of course, was inside the sleeping bag, wrapped like a Mexican tamale.

    I left San Carlos de Bariloche very early in the morning and headed south. It was snowing with great intensity. I was meeting a missionary group from a Presbyterian church in Canada, about 250 miles away. It took me two days to get there, due to difficult and uncomfortable weather conditions. Unfortunately, this group had left for Canada two weeks before my arrival. I stayed with a person who lived in a small house nearby, who was the person in charge of taking care of the Presbyterian facility. The next morning, I started driving back to San Carlos de Bariloche.

Winter in that part of the world was getting stronger than expected. The feelings of adventure, that throughout this trip had been controlling the reason, began to flit about in such a way that they literally pushed me to launch myself across the Andes Mountains, from San Carlos de Bariloche towards southern Chile in the middle of winter. Fortunately for the adventure, I did not have much knowledge about the road conditions at the top of the mountain range in that winter, but for the reason it was like a betrayal to the intelligence and to the prudence. Once again, the reason lost the challenge.

The first part of the ride to the top was nice, until I had to put chains around the tires. The road conditions were so bad that if I tried to describe it, I would begin to enter the territory of panic and terror. Visibility was conspicuous by its absence. It was difficult to see beyond two or three meters of the road, with the headlights of the truck. Not knowing how high it was, or how narrow the road was, made me drive so slow that it was sometimes difficult to feel the movement of the truck. I was concentrating on being as close as possible to the mountain, which I could touch by sticking my arm out the window.

There were many occasions where for several hours the left side of the truck was in constant contact with the snow and ice on the inside wall of the mountain.

To be honest, it was not a pleasant experience, at least until I started driving downhill via Chile. I spent two nights and almost three days inside the cab of the truck, experiencing the sensation of being an ice cream. Starting to enter Chilean territory from the mountain range was like opening my way to dimensions of Heaven that I had never imagined. There were lakes of all sizes –several meters in diameter to hundreds of meters in diameter – most of them surrounded by pine trees, rocks, and stones. There were countless small streams of water, half frozen, running down the hill and reflecting a diversity of multicolored patterns in the sunlight. That made me experience the divinity of creation beyond what my mind and heart were capable of perceiving. It was more than a fascinating experience – it was a spiritual communion with the love of Gaia, our Mother Earth.

After resting in the middle of this landscape for several hours, I started driving north to get to Santiago. The delight of driving through vineyards and villages along the way literally enriched my soul. Santiago, as a great city, was known mainly by driving through it. Later I took the road parallel to the sea, towards the mountains and the Atacama desert of northern Chile. This desert, at least the parts I traveled, was one of the driest places I had ever been to. The roads in the winter were not in good condition to continue on, so I headed towards the border crossing northwest of Argentine. This part of the Andes Mountains was also very beautiful. There were many ski resorts along the way.

Back in Argentina, the adventure again won over the reason, and letting myself be guided by my heart, amid the screams of my mind, I decided to go to Bolivia where I thought I could help the people there. I drove to Paraguay to take a small road that, based on the map, I assumed would take me to Bolivia through the mountains. Deep in the mountain, I found a small town of no more than three hundred people, most of them military with weapons. They were very friendly, and curious at the same time. Like so many other small towns that I had encountered during all those months, I thought that all these military men were mainly located there as part of government control of the mountains. I felt very good with them. After playing soccer, telling jokes, eating and sharing experiences with them for more than six or eight hours, they advised me not to continue my journey up the mountain. During the explanations of why I should not continue, they told me that they were all part of a guerrilla group and that it was not safe for me to continue. They had been watching me coming towards them for the last two days, and they told me they would watch me as I went back down the mountain.

For days I was thinking about the erroneous idea I had about the people involved with the guerrillas. At the very least, this group I shared with was made up of people who were very dedicated to their values, ideals, and beliefs. They firmly believed in justice and were quite convinced of what they were doing. Apparently they did not have any kind of remorse for what they were doing; on the contrary, they felt patriotic and that it was their life mission.

By then I had already been, for almost eight months, practically living among roads, small towns, and rustic places. I was tired, not only physically but also emotionally. The missionary experience that I had had in my mind before leaving Caracas proved to be only a magical and unreal illusion. I realized that I was truly an illusory, romantic and inexperienced medical missionary. The missionary work in my mind was what I had seen in movies or read in half-fiction, half-historical books. My feelings were divided between confusion and stupidity. At the time, I didn't know if the time I spent trying to be a medical missionary was of any significant benefit. In truth, I thought that somehow it was just a pretty crazy and risky adventure through South America. The exhaustion, frustrations, disappointments and perhaps the depression in which I was submerging myself, without knowing it, made me feel that all the risks taken were more towards stupidity and irresponsibility than towards the spirit of adventure in the missionary world.

Despite these feelings, which for me were nothing more than the product of the emotional, existential, physical, spiritual, human and professional shocks experienced over many months, within me there was joy, satisfaction and gratitude for everything I experienced, for the people I met and shared. There were gifts of life in the solidarity, friendship, culture, love, family, faith and divinity offered to me, without any interest involved, by so many people along my path –people who incorporated me into their lives as one more of them.

I think that perhaps I was not a missionary of staying, but of being. I could not stay as I wanted, but I knew that I was able to be as I wanted, and that of being able to be what I am, made me, in a certain way, a missionary of my own life mission.

I drove to Brazil, where I managed to find a place in the south of Brazil, near the Iguazu Falls, where a tugboat left for the city of Belem do para near the mouth of the Amazon River. With the help of several people, we were able to mount the truck among the cargo it was carrying. For about fifteen- eighteen days, we lived as a family team – the driver, his wife, a fourteen-year-old son, a seven-year-old daughter, my truck and I. We were able to navigate through a large number of small rivers to reach the Amazon River. During all that time shared, I undoubtedly improved my Portuguese and was able to teach them a little Spanish. In addition, as expected, I examined the whole family and left them a list of all the diseases and potential infections that they could suffer, the symptoms to recognize them and a number of treatments based on plants, tropical fruits, insects, and animals, as well as instructions for preparing different combinations of mud and plant mix for skin lesions.

I slept inside the truck, and we stopped in many small towns located along the small rivers. As expected, every night I ended up totally drunk from drinking his strong, homemade cachaca made with sugar cane. Drinking together was very important to them. They couldn't trust anyone who didn't drink with them to the point of getting drunk. For my part, I could not ignore my preventive medical mind, and I built a belt that circled my waist and between my legs, with an elastic band that I found in the tugboat. To this belt, I tied a rope that I had brought from Caracas and that was with me in the cab of the truck. One end of the rope was tied to me and the other to the axle of the truck. In short, I spent the trip as a garden dog. There wasn't much room to walk, and I had to walk around the edge of the tugboat. During the day it wasn't a problem, but at night, the action to marinade my brain in cachaca left my body to the fate of luck. Besides, the distance from the deck of the tugboat to the water was thirty to forty centimeters. Forewarned is forearmed.

In each small town we shared food with the local people, and we all ate together. The rest of the money that I still had, I divided into small amounts to give to the people with whom I shared all those days. It was a great feeling. In a way, I felt like I was the Santa Claus of the jungle. As soon as we reached a part of the coast of the Amazon River, about forty- sixty kilometers before the city of Belen do para, we transferred the truck to a larger tugboat that was leaving for Manaus. It was a quick, intense and high-quality farewell to my putative family, which left me with a sense of joy that was mixed with tears and smiles.

This new tugboat, where I was going to start navigating towards Manaus, belonged to a rather old, very nice man, around eighty-five years of age. We stayed overnight in the small boathouse, and the next day at dawn we began to navigate the Amazon River, heading west. It was a very uneventful ride. There was a boy, about seventeen to eighteen years old, who was helping the driver, and he literally did not like to talk. Not that he had autism spectrum syndrome, he was just grumpy. I think that in the five days that we spent navigating, we did not say to each other more than fifty words. He didn't even answer the "bom dia." It was literally a spiritual retreat for me. At times, I laughed just thinking of God's sense of humor towards me throughout this trip.

My thoughts, my feelings, my emotions, the memories of the experiences lived since my departure from Caracas, the unique magic of being navigating the Amazon River with its indescribable sunrises and sunsets, the darkness of the nights, the fascinating and amazing view of thousands and thousands of stars that covered the sky at night, the observation of flora and fauna, as well as many other things that escape me at this moment, all marked during those days an imprint of humanity within me, that I believe is still in my soul, in my heart, in my mind, in my day-to-day life and in the way I see and practice my profession as a doctor.

Navigating the Amazon in this type of boat allowed me to walk a few steps towards the bow and enjoy the magnitude of the sunrise, with a totally open sky and hundreds of birds crossing the horizon to the beat of countless sounds that came from the vegetation of the river banks. The harmony of colors and their reflections on the water made me feel that God was much more than what we as humans believe. The sunsets, meanwhile, I saw sitting on the roof of the truck, which was in the stern, with the front part a little bit out towards the water. The sunsets were different. In the midst of their indescribable beauty there was in the environment a feeling that nature was saying good night. Birds were flying low near the banks of the river, few sounds came from the vegetation that surrounded us, a hue in the colors that invited peace, the soft crying, the not thinking, and letting ourselves be carried away by the flow of life, and as soon as the sun went down, one was lost in the darkness of the night.

We arrived in Manaus without major mishaps. I stayed in Manaus for two days, around the dry dock where the tugboat left me, repairing some problems with the truck's brakes and buying supplies for the final crossing through Brazil to Venezuela. It rained very hard during those days. Still raining, I left Manaus minutes before it began to dawn. Despite the heavy rains predicted for several days in the north of Brazil, I decided to start my return to Venezuela. I did not know if I was already tired and wanted to return at all costs, or if that there was in me a feeling of confidence that the extraordinary luck that was accompanying me during every minute of this South American adventure was going to continue to manifest itself.

The road from Manaus to Boa Vista was really swampy, with many holes, mountains of mud and full of difficulties. Flooding from heavy rains disrupted the road in several places, causing me to take crosscuts through the surrounding forest. I was only able to advance no more than 140 to 160 kilometers per day. Around the third or fourth day, driving in very heavy rain with very poor visibility and trying to break through by taking shortcuts, I was stranded in a swamp well. I couldn't even open the door of the truck. When I managed to get out of the window, I fell into a mud pool, sinking to my waist. It was not easy for me to get out of this. I was half trapped and could hardly move. With my hands I was removing the greatest amount of mud around me. There was so much water that it took me almost an hour to get back into the truck through the window. There was not a soul to be seen around.

It really freaked me out quite a bit, and in a strange way a feeling began to invade me that this would be the beginning of the end for me. Hundreds of movie images of African jungles and safaris, where people were sucked into quicksand, kept passing through my mind. My plastic boots, my pants and my underwear were swallowed by the mud. I entered through the window of the truck, only dressed in a T-shirt. I was stuck there for two nights, praying that the truck would hold its own in the mud. Unfortunately, it was still sinking, albeit very slowly. With every movement, the creaks of the truck made me savor my heart. At noon on the third day, while in a half-asleep and half-awake state of existential trance, I began to hear voices in English.

The problem with being a neurologist is that the first thing that came to mind was that I was half delirious and beginning to have auditory hallucinations. Within a few minutes, I began to see a group of about five or six people, young men and women, no more than thirty years old, who were walking through the mud towards me. For a few seconds, I did not know for sure if I was alive, dreaming or dead. They looked to me like angels, with white skin and light eyes. The truth is that I was confused without knowing exactly what was happening. I remember laughing amid my nervousness, at the fact that "the angels" were speaking in English, if I was a Venezuelan surviving in a Portuguese- speaking country.

A minute or two later, behind them came a huge, rudimentary, camping-style truck with huge wheels. I began to shake as I thanked God, time after time, while an irresistible crying came over me. It took them about twenty minutes to get close to the truck. By then I was already mounted on the roof, yelling, "Thank you so much… thank you so much…"

They began to tell me that they were coming to help me and to stay calm, while they began to place iron plates so that they could get the truck out. They tied chains as best they could in the mud under the truck, to try to tow me. Their truck had two electric cranes in the front, which together with the backward movement, pushed the truck as it was mounting on the iron plates.

It took more than four hours until they managed to get me out. As soon as they took me out, I began to hug everyone, with tears in my eyes, thanking them for what they had done. Many of them saw me as a little weird. That night we camped together. I was so grateful, that I gave them all the provisions I had – food and drinks. For almost three hours I was giving medical consultations and healing skin lesions of many of them. All, or almost all, took the opportunity to have their own private medical appointment. It was a group of young people from Australia, New Zealand, Germany, Sweden and England, who were on an adventure tour through the north of Brazil. The people who rescued me were the two leaders and drivers, plus four volunteers.

Before arriving at the place where we camped, we passed by a roadside bar, a very primitive stall made of sticks and logs, where they sold cigarettes, liquors and uncooled beers. Of course, I told them to ask for whatever they wanted, without limits, without shame and without bashfulness. In the evening, I found out that they had bought large quantities of marijuana, among the cigarettes, spirits, and beers. Civilized Yanomami Indians were the owners of the bar.

All of them were sleeping in tents during their adventure trip, which each one assembled on their own. Most slept alone in their own tent, and only some shared it with a friend or partner. The truck they were riding in was fabulous – it was built especially for this purpose. In the front part, there was a large cabin where the drivers were, a space where they slept, in addition to the first-aid teams, etc. At the back were comfortable-backed benches with sturdy plastic-lined cushions, placed on either side. Each bench was for three people, and there was a corridor in the middle, like in an airplane. There were ten rows of banks, and in the back were large trunks where they kept each person's belongings. Below these trunks, there was a large space with doors that opened from the outside, where they kept the tents, folding tables, chairs, etc. On the sides and below the level where the passengers were seated, there were compartments with doors where they kept the water, the gas stove, the utensils, and where they stored the food. Really wonderful. From the floor, between the benches and the ground, there were approximately three meters of space. The iron plates that they used were kept in the lateral parts of the truck. The truck was very well equipped with all kinds of accessories. The drivers and leaders were two very determined women, both in their thirties. They were from the south of England. They explained to me about the tourist company and the different trips they were making around the world in inhospitable regions. There were seventeen in total, all with scars, multiple insect bites, sunburns and smelling like a tiger!

No need for more words –I was reborn.

The next morning I said goodbye to them, at least to those who were awake, with a feeling of gratitude that was far beyond their imaginations. I drove very slowly through areas of the road that were not greatly affected by the rain, to a military facility. The truck had no brakes, as the brake hoses had broken during the rescue. It only took about three to four hours. The military was very helpful. I stayed with them, sleeping in the truck for three days, while they fixed the damage to the truck. It took so long because the spare parts were being sought from other military posts. I ended up continuing the way back with no brakes on the right front wheel.

My trip back to Caracas took about ten more days. I was in such a state of spirituality with what had happened, that if there were difficulties, I did not see them or pay much attention to them or give them importance.

I did not imagine how much all these experiences had changed my way of thinking, of feeling, of acting and of speaking, until I landed on the reality that I had left behind almost a year ago.

I am convinced that the right to express our free will with freedom is part of our human condition, the right to embark on the adventure of questioning our beliefs, so later, by our own decision and not for the one of third parties, we can reject or accept them.

And those that are accepted make them part of our thinking, our feelings, our actions and our speech, with greater passion, commitment and intensity, redefining them according to what the moment in which we find ourselves of universal, spiritual, multidimensional and existential knowledge requires in favor of what we deserve as humanity.

Before ending this chapter on South America, I would like to thank "the life", for that extraordinary experience full of worldliness and spirituality, of pasts that mark presents and steal futures, of hopes that swing between the threads of faith, and of the cultural and religious impositions that deform our essence with the scars of their wounds, causing us to lose ourselves in the paths we take in our daily living. To that life that fills me with illusions and passions, with joys and sorrows, with securities and uncertainties, with laughter and tears, with dreams, with fantasies and with insomnia; to that life that makes me feel that I am a child of God and the essence of pleasure simultaneously, that I am virtue and wickedness, that I am harmony and chaos; to that life that makes me feel alive by making me walk hand in hand with death; to that life that is my life, that is your life, that is the life of the one I love and the life of the one that I do not like, the life of the one who I know and of the one who I have not had yet the pleasure of knowing; to that life that inclines me, in these moments, to dedicate these words that make me feel that I am life.

China and Pakistan

Five years after my return from South America, in July 1995, I was at the airport to begin to experience my second missionary adventure outside of my daily realities.

My natural weakness for venturing into the unknown led me to accept an extraordinary and different expedition. On this occasion, it was with a group of specialists in the areas of sociology, anthropology, and history. They needed someone with knowledge in the area of allopathic and holistic medicine, with experience in the management of children and the elderly. I really didn't know exactly what my role was going to be or what this group's true interest was in exploring the northwestern part of China and northeastern of Pakistan. But I decided to trust my instincts that were telling me that I should go. And from the moment I accepted the invitation until the moment of my departure, I only had the necessary time for the corresponding preparations. I said goodbye to my wife, Carolina, and my son, Ricardo, at the airport and went through immigration with a totally new feeling in my mind and in my heart, which brought up the circumstances I experienced at the beginning of my first missionary expedition. This time I felt calm, with a lot of self-confidence, with a pleasant optimism full of passion, positivism and, of course, a spirit of adventure. I was about to leave Caracas, via London, for Hong Kong, without knowing what I was going to find and with no one waiting for me in those lands. Just some instructions, names and addresses in Hong Kong.

The romanticism of my thinking and my feelings that I experienced at the airport and during the first hours of the flight, began to dissipate amidst the storms of hurricane winds that were invading my mind, my feelings and my emotions; products of memories and remembrances that were generating exponentially terrifying sensations of going back to the unknown, that I might not want to know. This only lasted a couple of hours, since a strange sense of security was growing inside me, simultaneously, that made me feel that I was prepared for a new different life experience.

The feeling was like starting the most important of all my graduate studies, where my professors and my consulting library would be the experience of trying to discover the feelings, the life intentions and the emotional-spiritual connotations in the environment and in the people with whom I was potentially going to meet.

In the midst of all this, my vanity and my ego became protagonists with illusions and delusions of grandeur, creating the fantasy that at the end of this new postgraduate scholarship, my diploma would say: "For having tried to discover realities of life, where all the realities are mixed in a confused synchronism, looking for their own truth."

I think I was kind of bored on the trip that I let my imagination recreate me. During those hours of thinking and feeling, the intention of arranging my thinking and my feeling in the attitude and direction of not trying to cling to any specific concept, thing or ideology, was reaffirmed in me, thus giving me more opportunity to find more easily the truth that I was supposed to be looking for, or at least find the way to where it could be found. On several occasions, I laughed alone at myself, at my naivety, and at the way I was using science fiction to put together romantic realities in my mind and in my heart.

Sitting for long hours on a 747 plane – which was totally full and with people of such varied cultures – made me think, in the middle of my illusory fiction, that I was in the middle of the jungle, a jungle different from the one I had experienced years ago, but with similar characteristics. While I was thinking about those jungles, the feeling came to me that all this potential life experience that was beginning to unfold was already known to me, that its memories were already inside of me without knowing it. The strange thing was the negativity that was trying to invade me, with thoughts and feelings that any new step forward would make the next step more difficult. Fear began to seize me without being able to avoid it.

My psychological defense mechanisms sought to compensate, hide or justify it by telling me: " "If I can't discover what I'm looking for, it won't change my happiness or my joy, since I will know what I don't need to look for in my life."

As the moment of landing at the Hong Kong airport approached, my heart began to stir memories, making me realize that what I was trying to do again had nothing to do with my intelligence or with my cognitive rational faculties, but with my crazy and strange feelings of adventure that I was sublimating by calling them human sensitivity. Perhaps they also had to do with my desire to fight to avoid falling into monotony and being absorbed by more of the same.

On the plane I prayed many times that the divinity in me and in others would help me learn to develop my sensitivity, in order to capture the goodness, the happiness and the beauty necessary to be creative and entrepreneurial in what was coming to me; as well as being able to develop enough humility to accept that in this search for new and different truths, I could have been wrong all my life.

I had a certain fear or strange anguish of not being able to see the coming reality as it really was, and not as I wanted it to be or wanted to believe it was. In those moments, my intention was to be able to touch the best of people, in order to find myself with their harmony, their peace, their happiness, and their love. I wanted to learn to be for them a doctor of hope, of knowledge, and a provider of peace.

In the constant wandering of my thoughts and my feelings from my brain to my heart and from my heart to my brain, I was beginning to realize that there was no need to go to any specific place in search of new truths full of happiness and peace, since all of them were perhaps already in us, waiting to be discovered and not necessarily in the outside world, like the one I was about to explore.

Landing in Hong Kong was a fascinating experience. The view of the city from the plane was incredible. The terminal was huge, beautiful and very modern, as well as being prepared to check hundreds of people at the same time. I was surprised by the technology. It did not take long for the adventure to begin to show its forms and intentions, nor for God to show his sense of humor, since after long minutes of waiting in front of the electrical baggage conveyor belts, and seeing all kinds of suitcases, backpacks, wrapped boxes, etc., I was faced with the inevitable acceptance that my luggage did not arrive, and after spending almost an hour in the middle of another group of people who were claiming in the middle of a disharmony of verbalized emotions, I was informed that my luggage was in London. Since I didn't have a reservation anywhere, I couldn't leave an address for it to be sent to me when it arrived. I had no choice but to wait until when the next flight from London arrived, which would be in about six hours.

I decided that the best thing was to go to the center of Hong Kong to find a room to stay, since it was daytime and it was going to be easier for me than waiting at the airport for six hours or more and taking the risk that it got dark, which could complicate things.

After having dealt with the pertinent procedures to get my luggage, I left the airport terminal, literally light, as the spirituals say, "light of luggage," only with my passport in my pocket. I went from the cool, modern terminal to the hot, humid and rainy Hong Kong environment. It was my first step towards reality.

In less than one minute of trying to catch a bus to go downtown, I was already soaked. It was like taking a shower with clothes on. This was one of those moments in life when one confirms how having money makes a difference. People leaving the airport took a taxi to their destination, and that is why they were smiling and dry. On the other hand, I, who took a city bus to go to my destination, experienced the sensation of being lost in a bowl of soup, since I was totally wet and mixed with all kinds of smells and essences coming from my environment.

Literally making faces and waving hands trying to give them a meaning, became my vocabulary. As is typical of a lost newcomer, I was trying to spot the YMCA building, where I was supposed to arrive, according to the instructions I had. The bad thing was that I did not have its exact address. After spending about two hours moving through the city center on the bus and getting stuck towards the back seats at each bus stop, suddenly, like a light opening in the sky, there was the lighted YMCA sign.

I felt like I had found the Star of Bethlehem. Trying to get off the bus was quite a psychiatric experience, from hysteria to agitation, from acute psychosis to claustrophobia, from frustration to anger, from despair to paranoia. After a couple of minutes I was able to get off, apparently without any significant psychiatric sequelae.

I entered the YMCA premises after walking several blocks in the rain. The first impression of the site was very pleasant, although I cannot deny that I was a bit surprised, as it was not what I expected. I thought these kinds of student facilities were more rudimentary. It looked like a very nice three- or four-star hotel. I registered by filling out a form and showing a special international missionary student card. I took the opportunity to find out if they could call the airport and ask if my luggage could be sent to the hotel, so that I would not have to return to the airport again. A very kind lady from the YMCA international office made the necessary calls and arranged with the airline to have my luggage shipped to me.

In my naive and weary thought process, the only thing that came to mind was how well Hong Kong people treated students. The room was quite nice, and after a long soak in the tub, with the subsequent usual nap until the water cooled down, I went looking for the people I was supposed to be traveling with by road in western China, Nepal and northern Pakistan for the next few months. At the address they had given me, no one knew them, and the odyssey began to try to find them. While receiving responses from the places in London, Islamabad, Beijing and Hong Kong, where I left messages, I took the opportunity to go to the Pakistani consulate to obtain a visa to enter their country. With two maps of the city, walking and using the underground transport, I managed, after several hours, to reach the address of the Consulate of Pakistan, and they gave me the same reception I had received at the YMCA.

To add a touch of enchantment to the welcome of my second missionary adventure, there was no Pakistani consulate in that direction. It was a police station. I tried to ask for the address of the Pakistani consulate there, but no one was willing to help me. Tired, hungry and soaked, I returned to the YMCA facilities.

Upon my arrival, my luggage had not yet arrived. I went to my room, dragging a strong, depressive feeling. I had some chocolates and cookies and fell asleep for a couple of hours. At midnight, I went downstairs to check if my luggage had arrived, which was supposed to have arrived at the end of the afternoon. The answer was a simple, "No, sorry." To make things worse, I had the bright idea of asking how much my room cost. In the midst of a unique half-Chinese and half-Chinese-English symbiosis, I discovered that the price of the room was $ 285 plus ten percent tax. After managing not to pass out, knowing that my budget did not allow me to spend more than forty dollars a day, on average, an Australian student, who saw the expression on my face, approached me and gave me the address of some cheaper places where I could stay overnight, in the central Hong Kong area. The YMCA hotel would keep my luggage there when it arrived, even if I was no longer at the hotel. After paying the bill for one day, I went out the next morning to check out the places the Australian had given me.

The affordable places in Hong Kong were unique, to say the least. The most viable of the alternatives was in a seven-story building. The first two floors consisted of a long corridor with tiny shops on either side, with very poor lighting, and hundreds of people walking and shopping that made it difficult to pass. Between two of these small shops were two stairs, with a large arrow painted on the ground just before the first step, indicating one to go up and the other to go down. The little hotel was on the sixth floor. Going up, people of different nationalities, mainly Chinese, Pakistanis, Hindus and Turks, were sitting on the steps of the stairs, smoking and drinking, wearing only underwear. They left a space between them to be able to pass. In the hallway on the sixth floor, on a door to the left, there was a sign "Chunking House." I rang the bell as directed, and an elderly Chinese woman opened the door. I tried to say in English, and with faces and hand signals, that I was looking for a room. The old woman didn't say a word, but she motioned for me to follow her. We started walking down a long, narrow, and very dimly lit corridor with small rooms on either side, separated by cardboard walls. I felt like I was walking in a prison.

The aroma that was distilled in the environment was etching its marks, not only in my nose, but also in my heart, my brain and my stomach.

The lady said in Chinese-English, " Sixty-five dollars," and with mimicry, I tried to tell her that I would come back later.

I left that place with an imminent and uncontrollable desire to cry and go home. When I went out into the street again, it was no longer raining. I started walking very fast, without a specific direction, perhaps because my thoughts marked the speed of my walking. After an hour or so, it started to rain hard again. Trying to protect myself from the rain, I entered one of the metro stations. Right at the entrance, there was a group of Chinese people eating what looked like a seafood grill. I decided to buy one. My romanticism and naivety vanished as soon as I put the first bite of that grill in my mouth. It was cold, weird, very spicy and full of tentacles. But the hunger was stronger than the taste and appearance, and in the end, everything on my plate went to my stomach. The burning sensation in my mouth prompted me to try to buy something to drink. I could not lose my missionary status, and especially the missionary budget that was very tight for the realities I was facing. Beers cost nine dollars; Coca Cola was six dollars; Ceylon tea cost one dollar. From that moment, Ceylon tea became my beers, my wines, and my Coca Colas. I did not try to find out, at any time throughout this adventure, what the Ceylon tea really was. Mind that does not know, heart, stomach and pocket that do not suffer.

After living the previous experience, I decided to return to the Chunking House, and I occupied the room assigned to me with a broad mind and a spirit of gratitude. As soon as I confirmed my room, I walked out to the YMCA facilities to look for my luggage that, thank God, had already arrived. Walking with my luggage on my back, I headed towards my new home. As soon as I got to my new home, I went to the community bathroom to wash my shirt, underwear, and stockings.

While waiting for an answer about my visas and the people I was supposed to travel with, I spent most of my time walking the streets of Hong Kong. The tourist part of Hong Kong was very nice and very clean. Every six to eight meters there were garbage baskets with their respective ashtrays for people to put cigarette butts. By the way, almost everyone smoked in Hong Kong. This area of Hong Kong was divided into two main parts – the island and the mainland. There were beautiful, tall buildings, incredible shopping malls, department stores, and a variety of four-fork restaurants mixed among five-star hotels. There were multiple and different walkways for pedestrians, decorated with transparent walls between hotels, shopping malls and department stores, which crossed the streets and allowed people to move freely in this area. At night, this area of Hong Kong offered a spectacular view of a unique scene of lights and colors.

From those walkways, during the day, you could see thousands of people walking from one side to the other, through the streets. Due to the dark color of the hair of the people of Hong Kong, it gave the appearance of thousands of ants moving at high speed. The metro trains did not have any separation between the cars, and the feeling inside was like being in a long tunnel in motion. Apparently, in that way, more people could be accommodated inside. The organization of the people inside the metro was incredible. As they entered, they sat in the available seats without leaving empty spaces –two rows of people sitting near the windows, and four rows of people standing in the hallway.

The platforms of the stations had arrows painted on the floor, which indicated the direction to enter and exit, allowing a faster circulation. Being inside the metro was like sharing the feeling of brotherhood of sardines after death –one on top of the other in a can.

The parks and squares were really beautiful, with different-colored flowers, water fountains and pagodas of different designs and sizes. In the open spaces covered with well-maintained grass, in the mornings and at night, you could see groups of about one hundred or two hundred people, of both sexes, in their 70s, 80s and 90s, gathered in a very organized fashion, all barefoot, and the men without shirts, doing Tai Chi. It was truly a unique scenery to observe.

After touring the tourist area several times, I walked towards the non-tourist area. Things in general were a lot cheaper, and all the signs and directions were in Chinese. It felt like there were a lot more people in this area. The feeling of adventure invaded my mind once more, and I walked into one of the popular Chinese restaurants.

There were approximately ninety round tables that could each seat twelve to fourteen people, and almost all the tables were fully occupied. Walking between the tables and looking for a free place, with my obvious appearance as an outsider, inevitably attracted the attention of most of the people in the place.

At that moment, I realized that it was not very often that a stranger entered this type of place, but I felt that there was no turning back. Between smiles, movements of my hands and repetitive movements of facial mimicry, a communication was created between the waiter and me. I could not know at what moment of the communication he understood what I wanted to eat. I know that he left laughing, and with him, many of the people at the tables laughed as he passed by. The wait seemed very long, since many eyes were constantly examining me from top to bottom.

About fifteen to twenty minutes later, the waiter arrived with the first course. It was a deep dish with a kind of cold jelly that had a strong, fishy smell. I felt like the guy who ate an oyster for the first time in human history! The second course was better. It was a tray of cold, white rice with a pasty appearance, accompanied by a handful of chunks of cold tentacles of octopus-like shellfish, in a spicy, red sauce. My hunger was the magic factor that allowed me to eat as much as I could.

When I was in my process of using the mimicry and movements of my hands to ask for the check, I realized that the waiter was angry with me, since he began to yell at me. The only explanation I could find was that he was angry because I didn't eat much. I tried to get to the door as fast as I could to pay the cashier. The truth is that I left that place half confused and half surprised.

On my way back, I crossed the tourist area. In a supermarket, I saw Haggen-Dasz vanilla ice cream. At that time, my missionary spirit was sleeping. I walked through the streets of the tourist part while enjoying the pint of ice cream. After enjoying those moments of ecstasy, I got home, and God showed his/her sense of humor again. There was a carnival in my room, with parades, troupes and even dancers, but no music.

It gave the impression that everyone in the neighborhood was invited. Families and children played and had fun between my clothes, the walls, the bed and even flew from one side of the small room to the other. I have never seen so many cockroaches of different sizes and colors put together, in my life. Trying to keep my heart inside my chest and my brain inside my head, I went to do mime to the lady in charge. She came to my room and started laughing and signed at me with her hands for me to stay there. She went looking for something, at the same time telling everyone she saw on her way something in Chinese that made everyone laugh. More than ten people returned with her to see my room, and seeing what was happening increased the intensity of their laughter. The lady began to spray the room with a primitive device. The smell was so strong that I had to wait almost two hours before going back to my room. I went for a walk to do self-therapy. When I returned, I found a broom next to the bedroom door. Upon entering the room, I began to sweep up the dead cockroaches that filled the plastic bin that was there. It was not easy at all to overcome the chills and nausea. Apparently my bedroom window was open and facing the garbage-dump area, and that was what had produced the Normandy invasion of the cockroaches.

After a few days of exploring Hong Kong and its suburbs of all kinds to the best of my ability, I was finally able to meet the leader of the expedition – a very strong English woman in her late thirties. She was very energetic and a good leader. Somehow there was a mutual feeling that we knew each other from somewhere.

After a while we had the opportunity to talk, and in an exchange of questions and answers, trying to decipher that mutual feeling of having met before, with an expression of joyful surprise, accompanied by a smile full of enthusiasm and a certain happiness that covered her face, she told me, almost screaming, that she was the leader of the expedition in northern Brazil that rescued me in the Amazon jungle several years ago. She remembered so many details and began to tell everyone around us all about it –from the red stain stuck in the mud (the truck was a red pickup that had a white cross painted on the roof of the cab and the white and red rear cabin) in the middle of the jungle, to the details of my facial expression thinking that they were from somewhere but not from Earth. At that precise moment, a sensation of chills invaded my whole body, and with tears in my eyes I knew that I was in the right place, but still without knowing why. I felt a sense of peace that was mixed with happiness and spirituality – difficult to put into words.

The leader instructed us to meet in two days on the outskirts of Hong Kong, near the coast, in the non-tourist area. The vehicle where we would go was parked in this area. There we would place our belongings in the vehicle and then go to the ferry terminal. The humidity and heat were really intense. The contrast between the tourist area and the popular suburbs was truly striking.

In the days that I had the opportunity to explore the Hong Kong area and its surroundings, trying to capture as much detail as possible, I learned that literally almost everything that moves or grows is eaten or sold in this part of China. All kinds of bugs, including cockroaches, all kinds of cold-blooded and warm-blooded animals, as well as any kind of entity from the plant kingdom were part of their eating habits. Here, as in other parts of the world, people who lived far from the big metropolis were significantly friendlier and more authentic.

A fascinating variety of kites, with different designs and colors, flew in the sky from any square or city park, guided by children and their parents.

Heavy intermittent rains were causing much damage in the areas that made up the first part of the expedition. The average temperature during the day ranged from thirty-six to forty-two degrees Celsius, with humidity balancing between ninety to one hundred percent. People with less economic resources were practically in their underwear. A strange and not very pleasant multi-aromatic smell, mixed with the smell of ashtrays full of cigarette butts, hung thickly in the environment. Unfortunately, in the region where the expedition was to begin, there were already more than fifteen million people who had lost their homes to the floods, and an unknown number of deaths and missing persons. It was a difficult reality, with nature continuing to show its power over the human race.

We left Hong Kong after sunset, by ferry, to the Guangzhou region. As was typical in the non-tourist area, the number of people on the ferry was something incomprehensible and even dangerous. It seems that there was no limit. People huddled anywhere available, and they sat on their belongings. The trip lasted about ten hours. The ferry made a stop of about two hours in Macau. I went down to walk around the area and took the opportunity to practice speaking Portuguese with some people. Upon arrival at the ferry port, we all left in the vehicle and headed to our destinations.

Since the beginning of the trip in this region, we could see thousands and thousands of people of all ages who traveled on foot or by bicycle. I was shocked to see so many people in their 50s and 60s with severe neurological sequelae from the golden age of opium.

Apart from the four who were involved in the project, we were accompanied by twenty-three other people from Europe, Australia and New Zealand, as well as a Chinese-English translator. The only logistics available was to join this adventure tourism group, headquartered in England. The characteristics of the vehicle in which we traveled were explained a little in the South America chapter. This vehicle, unlike the one in Brazil, had a Mercedes Benz engine, which, according to the driver, made it much more powerful. Sitting on the benches of the vehicle, I could see over the roof of the local buses.

A few hours after everyone had left in the truck, it could be seen that seventy to eighty percent of the vehicles in motion were bicycles and motorcycles. Avoiding flooded areas as much as possible, we started our journey to Wenzhou and then to Yanghson in the western part of China. The scenery of pines, ferns and hundreds of different types of trees of different colors and shapes, interspersed with the irregularities of the landscape that formed different terraces at different levels, designed in stone that rose to the top of the hills and mountains, was a unique experience of beauty and majestic nature.

The feeling was like being inside a National Geographic magazine. Yellow, brick houses with brown tiles, and a cement patio at the back for drying rice, adorned the sides of the road where we were going. Behind the houses were the areas for the cultivation of rice. They were filled with water as if they were natural pools, and their extension varied from hundreds of meters to kilometers, until they reached the crops at the foot of the hills and mountains. Hundreds of people working on them, with the typical cone hats, gave a special touch of magic in that part of the world. It was more than a landscape – it was a spiritual experience.

Many people and especially children of all ages were approaching our vehicle. It was impossible not to attract attention, since the size of it and the potpourri of different people who were in it, were in themselves an event. The happy faces, full of naive and welcoming smiles with an essence of innocence, where it seemed that their souls were expressing themselves, left me half hypnotized.

It was a beautiful and joyous scene. You could see people coming out from all over and of all ages, shouting, "hello, hello, hello!" They all wore light-colored clothing – white, blue-gray, or aqua green]. Only the main street in each town had asphalt.

After a few weeks in China, I had a better idea of what two billion Chinese living in this country meant.

The first 900 to 1000 kilometers of the route to reach Yangzhou were a fascinating experience – from the beauty of a field, without even a small place without a house, a patio, a tree, a river, a harvest or a moving bicycle, and the contact with thousands of people. They were such innocent people and so full of joy and energy. It was like living a Shangri-La moment.

Yangzhou was a great city, with the great majority of the constructions being made up of two or three floors, with the characteristic Chinese ornaments. There were lots of gardens and big trees everywhere. It was fabulous to experience taking a shower again, after several days on the road, sleeping in tents and walking through the markets among hundreds of people from the villages we passed. In those markets we bought what we needed for one day. Throughout this leg of the trip, I had the feeling of experiencing the essence of ancient wisdom of these fascinating people.

It was quite interesting to know that foreign people with white skin looked to them funny and comical, and they generally called us "big noses." The Chinese people, without any arrogance, were convinced of their superiority as a human race.

I had the opportunity to get to know the surroundings of Yangzhou by bicycle. It was a beautiful landscape with hundreds of hills and cone-shaped mountains – formed mainly of limestone – between rivers, trees and green crops. In the countryside, almost all women and girls, during working hours, walked along small paths between the crops and along the roads, carrying a stick on their shoulders with a basket full of vegetables and fruits at each end, which together with their long, plain dresses of different colors and their large typical hats in the shape of an open cone, offered the image of the China of the stories.

One night we had the opportunity to witness how they fished with cormorants. The fishermen went in small boats, with a kerosene lamp hung from a stake in the bow that allowed them to see the fish. Cormorants were tied with a rope around their necks, and they dived to catch fish that were getting stuck in their throats. They were coming out of the water and flying towards the boats where the fisherman would remove the fish from their throats. Each fisherman had four to six cormorants. After fishing for about five to seven hours, all the boats headed to the riverbank, where the women waited to collect the fish. On a sandy beach next to the barge dock, dozens of cormorants were standing in rows, one behind the other, all with their long wings spread out to dry them. It was incredible how so many birds could organize themselves so well.

As part of the project, they wanted me to try to obtain information about the medicine practiced in the suburbs of Yangzhou. With the help of the translator who was traveling with us, I had the opportunity to spend several hours with a healer in a small town on the outskirts called Funi. The healer was a typical Chinese old man with no teeth. He would sit on a small stool surrounded by all kinds of dead animals, such as: a wide variety of snakes of all sizes and colors, frogs, iguanas, birds of various sizes, etc. A large, clay pot of boiling water sat in front of him, and around him were many posters written in the local dialect about his special recipes. It was a unique experience sitting next to him, watching him prepare his recipes and listening, without understanding a word, to his ritual songs, as he dipped different combinations of animals into the boiling water for a few seconds at a time. The patient received a bottle of this water, paying according to the size of the bottle. I think this healer saw at least one hundred people, of all ages, in the period of about ten hours that I was with him. Once again, life was telling me that the secret of medical care was not based on the prescription given, but on the bridges of communication and bonds of trust that were created between the patient and the doctor.

Then I had the opportunity the next morning to visit the dentist in town. This was not easy for me. He was a man of about forty or forty-five years old, quite fat and with muscular arms. For me, watching him work was very grotesque. His work was mainly based on extracting teeth. The patients settled on a wooden bench and held onto a stake, which was driven into the ground, with their hands, placing their legs on each side of the stake. The dentist used a screwdriver and his fingers as work tools. When removing the piece, he threw it into a metal pot of water. After he finished with the patient, someone else sat down. In the meantime, the dentist half cleaned the extracted tooth between his fingers and placed it on a long table next to him, where there were hundreds of teeth – molars, incisors, and canines – from different people. When the patient was already settled in and holding onto the stake with both hands, he/she gave a signal, and then the dentist approached them from behind and flexed their heads back to perform his surgical procedure.

People passed by to look and laugh. It might have been that somehow there was a morbid attraction to all this. My complete lack of understanding of the spoken language may have contributed to my poor understanding of the situation. I was obtaining the information from these kinds of situations by observing and trying to guess the body language.

It was surprising how the majority of the adult population smoked unfiltered cigarettes. Also, during those days, I had the opportunity to familiarize myself with the use of the abacus. These simple instruments were like computers in the hands of these people, in relation to arithmetic calculations. In seconds they were able to multiply, subtract or add. My experience with the abacus was, unsurprisingly, at least a hundred times slower.

We continued our journey to the northeast, until we reach Huangguoshu where the largest Asian waterfall is located. The landscape began to change radically, due to the presence of a very dry area, where corn and sugarcane were the main crops. It was still amazing how they used every square meter of land. There was no place on land that was not used for some purpose. The nearly 1.4 billion Chinese who lived in that huge country by then made it look small in some way.

The way of life of those people was so simple and with so little technology or western influences, that it did not cease to amaze. Watching them prepare the fettuccini and linguini with rice flour was a unique and beautiful experience. On very long wooden tables, about a hundred men and women mixed the flour with water, and then they rolled out the dough with some rather rustic, long rollers, until they obtained a thin and flat layer. With a wooden bar that had many wires, separated from each other by about four to five millimeters, they cut the thin and flat dough along the table. These four-to-five-millimeter-wide strips were cut every two meters and separated from the rest of the dough. A group of people were hanging the strips of dough, as they were cutting them, on clotheslines in the front and back patios of the places of residence, as if they were wet clothes. Everything in China was extensive, and this artisan factory was not the exception. For several hours, driving along the only road in the area, you could see decorative ornaments of fettuccini and/or linguini hanging, practically without interruption. These fettuccini and linguini were later distributed among the families of the local communities.

Another interesting observation was the small number of children in the vicinity and almost no pregnant women on the street. The law imposed in 1990 only allowed one child per family, and if a family had a second child, the government would take him/her and give him/her up for adoption. This caused the pregnancy to be taken very seriously, so most of the pregnant women stayed indoors during that time.

From what one knew about the way in which the Chinese reproduced, in other countries where they had large families, perhaps this law could be explained. If China was allowed to freely reproduce, in a couple of decades the Chinese people would have no alternative but to invade the rest of the world, just to be able to move.

Continuing the journey north, the beautiful landscape began to be replaced by very dry and dusty mountains, where stones were the only decorative element. In the small towns along the road, in the midst of these dry and dusty landscapes, there were lots of pool tables placed in front of the residences and businesses along the main road. I didn't miss the opportunity to play pool with the locals every time we made a stop. It was great, since my communication with them didn't go beyond smiles, body language and touching us on the shoulders –which they seemed to like quite a bit.

Huangguoshu Waterfall was a true oasis in the middle of several days of desert mountains. In this area, the goat was the main source of food. Wherever we passed with the truck, or walking, we came across goat sales. Not very hygienic, but folkloric. Dozens of goats were hanging by the mouth, their extended limbs tied at the ends, giving the picturesque image of a mass crucifixion. In one place, forty to fifty goats could be seen in a row, belonging to a vendor. The vendors were placed without leaving much space between one and the other, along the roads and on both sides.

The human process of adaptation was so amazing that I was sitting on several occasions next to those goats, eating a part of one of them, without feeling remorse and without my stomach complaining.

We continued the trip to Dali, in Yunnan province. We stopped at Stone Forest to enjoy the countless limestone formations. Besides admiring the unique rock formations, I had the opportunity to share with many Chinese people who were coming from different parts of the country. We spent two nights camping in this area. The more I shared with local people and children, I was realizing more and more that there were no significant differences between people in general. It might have been that the cultural, ancestral and socio-economic situation made them look different observed from the outside, but inside, we were very similar, if not identical.

I did not miss the opportunity to enter a house if they invited me, or to drink or eat what they offered me. I was still fascinated by how we could share so many things, practically without using verbal language. Older men and women spent most of the day sitting outside their doors, smoking. I shared with many of them their smoking habits, although I did not smoke, but it was a great opportunity to establish friendship ties that I could not ignore. It was quite a procedure. In some sugarcane specially prepared for smoking, the interior compartments of the cane were filled with water. At one end of the cane they would put the unfiltered and homemade cigarette, and at the other end the smoke was inhaled through the mouth and the nose. I think they invited me to smoke wherever I was walking, to laugh at me and with me, since my cough was accompanied by tears and strange grimaces, which I could not avoid with each inhalation of the smoke. Between laughs, I was creating a communication with the local people that made me feel welcome. Many people crowded around to see how I survived each puff of smoke. My throat and lungs remembered those moments for several days later. The faces of the toothless old men who laughed at me were a true poem of life.

A few kilometers before reaching the city of Kunming, we had an accident. A van full of people crashed into our huge truck. My medical reflex was to jump out of the truck to help the people. Without even really realizing what I was doing, I ran to pull bleeding and screaming people out of the van. The people who were helping communicated with me in broken English. In a magical way it seemed that we understood each other perfectly.

After a few minutes, I found myself surrounded by hundreds of people before the police arrived. Thanks to my spontaneous reaction, I spent around seven to eight hours in a local jail until the expedition leader, with a local translator, could explain the situation by saying that I was an American doctor, etc. The jail, by the way, was not too bad. It was a bit crowded, but I sat in a corner and remained there, sleeping most of the time.

Until the problem in which the truck was involved was solved, we stayed in Kunming. Here I was really able to explore every corner of the city and run into countless people. The first thing I did was buy clothes like the ones the locals wore, to try not to attract too much attention on my exploratory walks. It was not difficult for me, since it was practically the same design for men and only in two colors – dark gray or brown. I felt like a sponge, absorbing information everywhere. At dawn I was already walking around to get in touch with the workers, then I walked through the artisan shops and humble residences. I ate what the local street stalls sold, like everyone else. Many times it was impossible for me to go unnoticed, and at other times I believed that I was going unnoticed.

In that region of China, I was able to observe manifestations of ancient Chinese ideas of beauty. There were families that still thought that small feet on a woman were a sign of beauty and royalty. Female members of these families, as soon as they were born, had their feet bound in a forced flexion position, with the idea that their toes would move closer to the heels, significantly reducing the size of the foot. It was very easy to recognize them by their strange and peculiar gait.

The lonely, desert mountains were spectacularly illuminated by millions of stars that spread their brilliant reflections through the dense darkness of night.

After several days, we continued on our way to Dali. This city was a stepping stone back to a great city, with all the typical Chinese characteristics: pagoda-style temples, statues, beautiful flowers and fascinating gardens. This break on the trip allowed me to regain the feeling of being clean. The public showers were fabulous – you could spend hours under the hot water. But the most important thing was the great opportunity to be mixed with so many people. Of course, waking up before dawn and walking out exploring even the tiniest place, trying to make contact with people, gave me the inevitable title of crazy, big-nosed tourist.

By the way, I did not know that they called me that, until, in one of my walks, I passed near the group's translator, and he approached me, laughing, and told me that they called me that wherever I went. I saw it as something fabulous and very positive, since I could tell that there was some communication. But I confirmed to myself, that no matter how much I dressed like them, I did not go unnoticed, even though I also wore a hat like the one they used.

Being mixed with them and constantly walking along all kinds of sidewalks, helped, in a way, to sow a certain spirit of routine, which apparently generated a strange confidence, which made it easier for me to spend hours and hours among the humble local houses, smoking, drinking, eating and performing all kinds of body expressions to establish the best possible type of communication with local people. Stares at me and smiles were the main responses I got. From time to time, and especially women and children, came up to me, laughing. Women touched me, and children played with some of their homemade toys. With men, most of them elderly, communication was based mainly on looking at each other's eyes and faces, while we were smoking or drinking together. The more I smoked and drank with them, the more willing they were to invite me into their homes and introduce me to their relatives.

The expression in English, "When there is a will, there is a way," became a reality for me, and I'm sure for many of them as well. We found our unique way of communicating. Of course, by nightfall I was already super dizzy from smoking so much and half-drunk from drinking so much, but I was able to manage, without many mishaps, to walk through the rudimentary and tiny spaces between the houses in the direction of where we were camping.

I did not know what they were thinking or what they were talking about, but there was joy and laughter in the surroundings and an invitation for the next day.

The Alka-Seltzer and club soda were my best companions in the evenings and really helped to stop the spinning twists of my tent. My stomach was the one that was not very happy with what I was doing and was really protesting.

The local customs, their typical clothes and their special welcome to try to get to know us a little, made those days in Dali a part of me, their continuity in time being left to the discretion of my memory.

Their human qualities, their nobility, their wisdom, their joy and their unique and special idiosyncrasies made them extraordinary characters. We learned to say, "Thank you, friend" – "Xie xie, pengyou" – in each other's language, which we repeated almost as the only form of verbal communication. Although it was forbidden to have any kind of physical contact in public, some of them ran up to me just to touch me for a few seconds or to offer me a souvenir, which was food most of the time. I was constantly amazed, not only by how much we could communicate without speaking, but also by the beauty of these people.

One of the things that was most difficult for me to adjust to was those people's habit of spitting on the ground around them with great frequency, up to one or two times a minute. Their smell and other aspects of their personal hygiene were accepted without generating any kind of reaction.

We restarted our journey towards Lijiang located at 3,400 meters above sea level, near the Jade Dragon Mountain (7,150 meters) and the Tiger Gorge (7,300 meters). The road was not easy at all, because of its narrowness, the cliffs, and because of its sandy condition with stones and holes. The Chinese minority, known as the Naxi, lived in this area. They had very typical characteristics, most of them dressed in blue, with black hats in the Russian style. The women carried their baby in black bags on their backs. At the front door of their single-story brick homes, most of the family members spent their days talking, smoking, and eating. I spent many hours like a salesperson, from door to door, with the intention to get to know them a little. Unfortunately, they kept themselves to themselves and didn't smile much. In addition, they did not show any type of interest in participating in anything other than their immediate relatives at home. The physical environment in which they lived was shared by a highly diverse community of rats and mice of all sizes.

In some areas, there were people who were more involved with the environment. Children played with dragonflies. At the end of a thin bamboo stick, they tied many ropes. At the other end of the ropes, dragonflies were tied around the belly. They raised the sticks and enjoyed watching the dragonflies flying around the stick. They obtained their dragonflies near water, in fountains or ponds. With a unique ability, making quick movements with their hands, they grabbed them in their flights and put them in their mouth, leaving the tail outside their mouth. In this way, they were able to tie them to the ends of the ropes. The more dragonflies they had, the more prestige they acquired. Those with the most dragonflies were applauded by people passing by. There were children with ten or twelve dragonflies tied at a time. Dragonflies flew in many directions trying to get loose, which they did quite often.

All kinds of very unique, homemade stringed musical instruments and mandolins, made of metal plates of different shapes and sizes, were played everywhere almost constantly.

To try to share with a part of the local population that lived in small towns located along the Tiger Throat and on the Jade Dragon Mountain, I joined a trekking. It was a small group of about eight to ten people with me. When we reached 4,500 to 4,700 meters, my body began to complain of the altitude, and a headache, dizziness, nausea and shortness of breath began to be my companions on this trekking trip.

In certain areas, the paths were so narrow that, added to my fear of heights, I passed them by crawling across the ground, with my head down, seeing no more than thirty to forty centimeters of the road in front of me. Having to drink water often to prevent, as much as possible, the mountain sickness, made me even more dizzy and nauseous. During those few days of trekking through that gorge, I understood very well the need to know my limitations. On two occasions I almost "don't tell it anymore." The huge cliffs and my fear of heights took with them my concentration and coordination, causing me to lose my balance on the narrow paths. Thank goodness I was tied with ropes to six other hikers who saved me. In those seconds that I was left half hanging towards the precipice, my life passed before my eyes at such a fast and strange speed, that in seconds I felt I had seen decades of my life. That vision of my earthly life left me with a feeling, after being rescued, that I was doing something wrong and incorrect, and that I was in the wrong place. Those days were of very intense meditation on me and on my life. I was half confused for several days afterward.

The dozens of beautiful blue pools of water and lakes, surrounded by long stretches of flowers, mainly camellias, throughout my tour of the Jade Dragon Snow Mountain, gave me the feeling of being in Heaven. For many days I literally walked along the Yangtze River, the longest river in Asia – 4,200 kilometers.

Two days after returning from the excursion, we resumed our journey to the northwest. Now we were heading towards Kunghiayu, and then heading towards Chengou, in Shighua province.

In this province of Shighua, I had the great opportunity to see all kinds of transport vehicles – from one, two, three or four-passenger motorcycles to all kinds of primitive cars pulled by bicycles, animals, tractors, and people. All of them were driving between cars and buses of all sizes.

Multiple varieties of mixed Islamic and Chinese pagodas were part of the landscapes of this region. People were different. There were many Islamic Chinese, and they had different eye colors and facial expressions. They did not have the naive and innocent expressions that were seen in the thousands and thousands of people during the first months of this adventure. These people seemed more oriented to doing business and making money. I had the opportunity to attend the annual rural fair, where thousands of people from this province gathered to do business with their animals – mainly horses, donkeys, and mules. It was another unique experience. The malicious human weakness was progressively invading the spirit of the vast majority of sellers, in a strange and almost unbridled struggle to try to deceive and cheat, with the sole intention of obtaining more money in each transaction. Every five to ten meters of this huge dusty esplanade, there was a fight or a strong argument. Of course, I did not understand a word of what was being said, but the body language at the time was of universal understanding.

Due to large landslides caused by floods, which interrupted the road in several sectors in quite significant dimensions, a section of the trip had to be made by train. Previous floods had destroyed several hundred miles of rural roads, and the only way to get to Chengdu was by train. Of course, our gigantic truck came with us on the train. The experience inside the train was something like a miniature China Town Ghetto. The absence of good manners reigned everywhere – people spitting everywhere. Most of the people were in their underwear, as the humidity was close to 100%, and the heat was suffocating. The temperature at night did not drop below thirty-five degrees Celsius. There were people everywhere, including families with children on the floor, along with people drinking and smoking while playing cards or dominoes. I sat in the same corner that I found when I arrived, for the entire sixteen-hour drive. I had no doubts about the opportunity to experience Chinese suburban culture. I got a good dose.

Chengdu was a place to visit monasteries and learn about the different types of Buddhas. The people here, as in any other big city in the world, were mostly indifferent and slightly aggressive. This city had a little more than twelve million inhabitants.

I had the opportunity to witness again one of the many paradoxical things that happen around people, medicines and the fear of contracting a disease. One of the four of us who came to this project – the sociologist – who was extraordinarily obsessive-compulsive in taking prophylactic therapy to avoid malaria, contracted malaria. Until now, no one else had presented any type of symptoms that made one suspect the diagnosis of malaria.

Our travel companion, unfortunately, began to present episodes of chills that made his whole body shake, accompanied by a fever that was increasing rapidly in a matter of hours. In the midst of all this, what he was telling me was that his stomach hurt a lot. As soon as the fever started to go down, he fell asleep and began to sweat profusely. Knowing the personage, I stayed by his side the whole time, until the symptoms disappeared. At the end of that attack of malaria, I convinced him to go to a hospital in this city, since it was important to know the type of malaria. Fortunately, the malaria he contracted was not the aggressive type caused by Plasmodium falciparum. After two days in the hospital, he continued the journey with us, and I took care of him from the medical point of view. Everyone else in the vehicle, except me, started taking prophylaxis almost as obsessively as our friend. The reason I didn't take it was mainly due to the side effects and my unique tendency to stay away from drugs and doctors as much as possible. Also, it was easier for me to balance the fear and uncertainty components associated with malaria.

One of the best, unique and very special experiences of this expedition was having the opportunity to spend several days at the China Research Institute, where nineteen panda bears lived. Panda's babies are so fragile and small that they are kept in an incubator with the same type of feeding and care as any baby in a Neonatal Intensive Care Unit of a hospital in a big city. Its size at birth is about twelve to fifteen centimeters, and they have transparent skin that allows you to see the red color of the muscles. Its eyes are closed, with a transparent membrane, and its mouth opens just a centimeter or less. The rutting period is around August-September. Generally, each captive mother has two cubs, and one of them dies in the first hours after birth. During my stay, there were three puppies in incubators. In an open facility, there were four panda cubs, each about eleven to twelve months old. These puppies were fifty-five to sixty centimeters tall and weighed forty to forty-five kilos each. They were extraordinarily playful. On several occasions I was able to play with them. Their fur was tough like nylon. The first time I stroked them, I had a strange sensation, mainly because I had in my mind the feeling that I was going to touch a teddy bear. But the thrills of having this unique and fortunate opportunity far outweighed any previously learned feelings.

The adult pandas sat down for most of the day, eating bamboo. They really did look like the big teddy bears in toy stores. Of the forty different types of bamboo, those pandas only ate the one known as arrow bamboo, and each one of them ingested between forty and fifty kilograms of bamboo a day. Their weight varied between 100 and 150 kilograms, and their lifespan was around forty years. Their daily schedule was ten hours eating, twelve hours sleeping, and two hours playing. What a life!

When they played, the large pandas hugged each other and did cartwheels several times. Sometimes the larger pandas hugged the smaller ones and twirled and tumbled together. The little ones made a sound similar to that made by children complaining. The big pandas had much softer fur than that of young ones.

There were only forty-nine panda bears in the institute, and in the mountains, about one hundred kilometers from the institute, was their sanctuary. Only people from the institute were allowed to enter the sanctuary. There were around one hundred more pandas there. In China, they were doing their best to preserve these beautiful bears that were on the way to extinction. The person who killed a panda bear was sentenced to death by hanging in a public place. In the institute, there were hundreds of lesser pandas, or red pandas, that looked like a cross between a panda and a fox. The feces of panda bears was crescent shaped and did not give off any kind of smell.

They were several unforgettable days, not only for the unique learning experience sharing, caring for, playing and feeding the panda bears, but also for sharing with the beautiful people that made up the institute's work team. They had a special spiritual focus in their work that generated a mystical atmosphere around the institute. The magic of these pandas was special, and the magic of the people who worked with the pandas flirted with the divine.

We continued our journey north to Sichuan. On the road, there were so many people in wheelchairs that it was somewhat alarming. Most of them had a bicycle system attached, with the pedals up to be able to travel by moving the pedals with their hands. About eighty percent of people were travelling by bicycle. It was amazing to see hundreds and maybe thousands of bicycles parked together in the center of the big cities of this Sichuan province.

The road was very dry, and it was through several desert mountains 3,500 meters above sea level. The narrow roads and cliffs kept my mouth shut for most of the journey, mainly to prevent my heart from leaping out of my mouth in its runaway acceleration.

Thousands of apple trees were mingling among the deserted areas. After two days, we arrived at a beautiful mountainous landscape full of trees with green, yellow, brown and red colors mixed in a unique harmony – an autumnal picture in the middle of summer. Between the mountains were meadows traversed by rivers of great flow, with waters of white and blue colors that wound their way between beautiful expanses of yellow flowers and crops of golden wheat. It was like getting to Heaven after coming from Purgatory.

We headed to Jiuzhaigou National Park to camp for a few days and to prepare ourselves to start crossing the Northwest-China desert. The typical hairy cattle, known as yaks, were the transport vehicle of the local population at that height. I had never seen yaks. When they started showing up along the trail, I was sitting in the back of the truck in the space open, facing outside, and I was half asleep and half awake. In the middle of my reverie, I thought how great the cows were around here that had tails and manes like that of horses. When I woke up, that was what I saw –rare cows with tail and horsehair. They were the famous yaks.

Those hairy bulls and cows really smelled, or rather, they stunk. From the moment I came into contact with them, their scent accompanied me twenty-four hours a day, despite all attempts to avoid it or hide from it.

Within a few hours of camping 4,000 meters above sea level, I began to experience a constant headache, associated with inevitable fatigue. The nights were very windy and cold, and my tent was tropical. I slept like those sausages covered with corn dough – corn dogs. I was the sausage, and the corn dough was the two sleeping bags I had. On the inside roof of the tent, my perspiration freezing like drops of ice. The sound of the movements of the tent with the winds kept me awake most of the night. Several times at night I had to go out to re-secure the ropes that came loose. Every time I went out, I saw more than one fellow traveler doing the same thing.

Staying emotionally stable in the midst of that difficult loneliness was not easy.

I spent three days walking and enjoying the Jiuzhaigou National Park, without losing the opportunity to observe the people that I met on the road, while trying to communicate with them. With many, communication was nothing more than a "hello" in both directions.

At dawn, we continued our journey. We began to cross a long stretch of land between the mountains, known as "grassland." They were extensive prairies, or as they would say in Argentina, "pampas." Those meadows could be any golfer's dream. They looked like golf-course savannas, where, instead of golfers, there were yaks of all sizes, and instead of clubhouses, there were small camps of Tibetan immigrants.

The clothes of these Tibetan immigrants were very peculiar. They wore their clothes all day and all night. They took it off to change it with the changes of season, and for that they did specific rituals. The pants were loose bloomers, tied at the waist and ankles. They had an opening between the legs. These pants were worn by all – men, women, boys, and girls. Their physiological needs were fulfilled through these openings.

During the times shared with them, mainly when we were inside their large, circular tents, their activities were quite peculiar. For example, men and women had intercourse in front of everyone else. Without taking off the clothes, the man stood behind while they both crouched down. The strangest thing was witnessing those scenes, while conversing, through our interpreter, with the leaders who invited us one day to eat in their tent. That night, we were standing near the food that was being prepared, with a fire in the center of the tent. About seventy to eighty people lived in each tent. It seemed that there were no specific families, but instead they all formed a single large family. The smell of the people and inside the tent was so strong and different that I did not try, at any time, to identify where it came from or what it was like. My digestive capacities weren't ready to handle that information.

With them, without knowing it, I ate dog meat that they offered me. It was meat that was roasted on the brick stoves in the center of the store. It was a very dry meat, without much flavor, overcooked and tough. They gave me pieces in my hand, and I ate it like they did. Everything was strange. It was like experiencing a parallel life. I knew where I was and what I was doing, and at the same time I feltlike I didn't know where I was or what I was doing.

I found out about the origin of the meat when after hours of sharing with them, the camp cook, according to what I understood through his body language, asked me to follow him to show me their food storage. I was so unconscious of what was happening, that I followed him, almost like a reflex. Beneath the tent was a large underground room, like a large cave. When we got to the back of that cave-room, there were many dogs, around sixteen to twenty. The smell was horrible, and while he was talking to me and saying things that I could not understand, he took one of the dogs, and with a big, curved knife cut its neck, pouring its blood into a large, wooden tray at the same time that he began to peel off its skin. The connotations of having eaten dog meat vanished almost instantly, at the horrible scene of having seen that poor dog killed.

The "wow" factor really got me. I was left quite confused, in the midst of feeling very dizzy, while trying to do my best to deal with the nausea. Respect for their idiosyncrasies clashed head-on with a feeling of helplessness and inaction, which grew by leaps and bounds within me and made me feel like a coward for having done nothing to prevent the dog from dying in that way. It was not easy to quickly unlearn what I learned in my life, so that this would not take away my freedom to experience what I was experiencing without judgment or prejudice, and without breaking the atmosphere of fellowship that we were generating on both sides.

We had already shared about three to four hours with them. When we returned to where we were, in front of the dog grill, I motioned for the translator to begin the process of saying goodbye. This whole process flowed smoothly and with joy. We said goodbye to the vast majority of the hosts, while I tried to prevent my newly generated emotions from overshadowing my thoughts, my feelings, my actions, and my humor. I did not tell the translator about the meat we had eaten, since he had eaten quite a lot and had apparently enjoyed it. Perhaps because he thought, like me, that it was yak meat. Of course, everything that happened between the cook and I was unable to be put into words, until many years later.

After a long night in my tent, mainly due to insomnia caused by a mixture of many mixed feelings, the next morning we continued our journey. The road continued uphill. Around 5,000 meters above sea level, breathing became a bit more difficult for me, and the dizziness and headache were already constant. All this was accompanied by sensations of tingling and needle pricks in my body, which were self-designated as my travel companions, which, with great passion and intensity, were courting me twenty-four hours a day.

Following resting for a day, in a town called Lungmussi, to adapt to the altitude, we continued our journey to the north of Pakistan through the "Karakorum highway." That was the highest road in the world at that time –between 4,800 to 5,100 meters above sea level]. This road, about four to six meters wide and about seven hundred kilometers long, was built by the people of Pakistan and China, between northwest China and northeast Pakistan. It took fifty years to complete, and many people died due to local earthquakes and landslides. This primitive road, built by hand, allowed us to cross into

Pakistan in about seven to eight days. Apparently, that was the best time of year to cross it.

We stayed for a few days before taking the Karakorum road into a Tibetan village of approximately 4,000 people. Almost ninety-eight percent of them were monks. There were many small monasteries, and around them were dozens and dozens of prayer mills or prayer wheels. They consisted of hundreds of carved-wood or copper-brass cylinders that rotated on a central axis. Those cylinders had mantras inscriptions all over their surfaces. They were arranged in a linear fashion. The monks rotated them in the same clockwise direction. Those prayers filled them with wisdom and purified the negativity of their karmas. The monks spent many hours of the day rotating around these great rows of cylinders. Some were singing, others with their heads down muttering prayers, and others, every couple of meters, knelt and lay face down with their arms outstretched.

All the monks were going in the same direction. For some reason, I walked in the opposite direction to see them head-on, to observe their faces and their gestures. I was very alert to everything I was experiencing, trying at all times to be very discreet, so as not to fall into disrespect. At no point did I try to touch the cylinders while they were praying. Only when no one was around did I approach them to see the inscriptions, the copper and the woodwork. Of course, at no time did I try to take pictures of the monks, or of the sites they considered sacred. Before taking a photograph, I asked permission, with great respect. Very few photographs were taken.

There were monks of all ages, including some 600 to 800 children between the ages of five and fifteen. I had the great opportunity to see hundreds of monks, on several occasions, all walking barefoot and praying around the monasteries, touching those prayer wheels. The town was almost literally inhabited by male humans. There were no female monks.

All the monks wore very aromatic, purple-red robes, and all had their heads completely shaved. The kids looked great with their bald heads, red robes, and walking barefoot. The children always hung out together in large groups. On two occasions, to different groups of them, I tried to reach out and was immediately surprised by their aggressive rejection response. I watched them for several hours, at different times and in different places in town. And their aggressiveness continued to surprise me. They played with each other, pushing each other. In those nasty games, many fell and were hit. When that happened, the rest of the children stood around the one who was being beaten, laughing at him. As soon as some older monk caught their attention, like little robots they modified their behavior by grouping themselves in rows to continue on their way.

The monks walked in pairs, holding hands, and greeted each other with kisses on the cheeks. On young monks it looked natural, but on older monks it looked a bit grotesque. I had several opportunities to have a conversation with a group of young monks. The vast majority had a certain vocabulary in English, and they understood it quite well. They spoke of the many problems they were experiencing by spending their entire lives segregated, only surrounded by men in rather primitive conditions.

With that group of young monks, I had the opportunity to get to know the temples and monasteries of that region from the inside. Almost all of those temples and monasteries were built of beautifully carved wood and decorated with rugs on the inside. The walls and ceilings were decorated with silk fabrics painted with figures of different Buddhas. On the back wall of the temples were several statues of the Buddha and posters of the Dalai Lama. Mixed with the painted figures of Buddha were paintings of grotesque and horrible scenes of animals, such as monkeys, tigers, wolves, etc., devouring and eating human beings; monster faces; scenes of physical aggression between animals and humans, etc.

On the perimeter of the town and on the top of the surrounding mountains, there were many very tall poles with flags of various sizes and different colors – green, blue, white, red, and yellow – where prayers were written for the wind to carry them away to heaven.

As part of their rituals, they threw small papers of different colors, with prayers written on them, against the wind, for the same purpose as the flags. Sometimes they set the papers on fire before tossing them into the air.

Heavy rains and bad road conditions significantly slowed down our trip. There were days when we spent many hours just to travel a couple of kilometers. The prolonged daily physical exertion trying to get our truck out of the multiple mud traps really exhausted me physically. At times I was so physically exhausted that I fell asleep with my legs in the mud and my arms holding the thick ropes used to pull the truck.

Almost literally at the speed of a turtle, we made it to Xiahe. In that part of China, the majority of the population was Chinese Muslim. They were taller than the rest of the Chinese we had seen. Both men and women covered their entire bodies with dark clothes, leaving only their faces exposed. After spending several days in the same wet and muddy clothes, wearing thick raincoats to protect myself from the cold and rain, and sleeping from time to time, as I mentioned earlier, I was able to experience the unique and pleasant feeling of being under the water of a shower as soon as we arrived in Xiahe. It was a primitive and rudimentary shower but good enough to allow me to be under it. The water was cold, but at the time it didn't matter much.

Xiahe was a small town with a population of approximately 25,000 habitants, at about 3,900 meters above sea level and surrounded by green mountains. A high-flow river, about twenty-five to thirty meters wide, crossed the town longitudinally. It was scary to approach the river where the brown water was running at high speed, making waves. The heavy rains of the previous weeks had brought the river to the alarming level of flooding. Thank God the rain stopped, and the river started to go down in the following days.

In that town there were also many Buddhist monasteries. Among them was the Labrang Monastery, the fifth largest in China. Throughout the town were extremely long walls, several hundred meters each, with inscribed copper barrel rollers – prayer wheels or prayer mills – lined up on both sides of the walls. The average length of the walls was around two hundred meters. Local people were walking alongside them, touching them while praying. In that place there were many people, who were not monks, who knelt or lay in the dust, with their arms and legs extended almost in front of each of those barrels.

In one of my walks, I tried to calculate the number of cylindrical rollers that were around the town. There were about 6,000, more or less. During the bows, they were holding, in their hands, circular rosaries of different colors. Every day, every citizen of that village, monk or not, walked around those rows of holy rollers, praying for at least five to six hours.

With the past experience, I contacted some young monks who were interested in making conversation. With a group of five monks, I spent most of the day during the time we were in the city. They were super curious, and they spoke and understood English quite well. The six of us walked all over the place together, and they all were accepting that I invited them to meals, which they enjoyed very much, in addition to teaching me to eat all kinds of local food. At the end of the afternoon, the five of them were leaving for the Labrang Monastery, where they lived.

On the third day, they invited me to participate in their daily activities within the monastery. The decoration of the halls or temples for the ceremonies was similar to that of the temples that I had visited the previous week in the Tibetan village. In this monastery, all the Buddha statues were painted in gold. The columns, walls and ceiling were covered with multi-colored decorations. Lines of cushions covered the floor. These cushions were located in such a way that the monks could sit facing each other. Between two rows of cushions were narrow corridors, where three rather older monks and three guardians walked during the six-hour ceremony, reviewing the monks' prayers. The guardians were dressed in very beautiful and lush costumes, with large metal shoulders and sophisticated hats made of gold and silver.

They carried some very well-decorated, long rectangular sticks or canes, with which they hit the wooden floor next to the monks who were talking or making noises.

The sharing with them brought many concerns. There were so many monks of different ages in their rooms, including children, sleeping on the floor in the same room, so crowded that it was impossible not to touch each other while they slept, besides not being able to see where each one was, due to its night darkness. All this added to the intense smell of sperm in the community rooms, which was impossible to avoid. The mystical impression obtained in the ceremony that I had participated in at the monastery was destroyed, and was replaced by a strange sensation of being in the middle of a precarious grotto of male prostitution.

These monks lived in great disorder, and their rooms were smelly and disorganized. At the main doors of the temples, they left their typical boots lying everywhere.

What impressed me the most in that town were the cemeteries. At the top of the surrounding hills and mountains were simple temples, in the shape of a wedding cake, built with cement and without decorations. The tiers ranged from about five to seven meters in diameter at the base, to about two to three meters in diameter at the top. Each monument had four to six levels, following the distribution of traditional wedding cakes. Scattered among the stands were hundreds of corpses torn to pieces and scattered among shoes and clothing. Dozens of raptors, vultures and Turkish vultures celebrated their daily feast there. Rats of all sizes pulled clothing, and human flesh was everywhere. Clouds of flies and strange insects were flying and buzzing. There were old and new corpses mixed up.

The smell was indescribable. I've never smelled anything like this before.

I was in shock for several minutes, and I survived the sporadic nausea and vomiting, but I didn't want to miss any details of that unique and horrifying scene. Those memories have been manifesting on a conscious level in my mind, intermittently, ever since. Thank God that over the years, the frequency of those memories has decreased significantly. For many months, the idea of the lifestyle of those Buddhists that I had been observing was fighting between reason and acceptance. In the midst of that conflict, a feeling of disappointment was planted in me. In my constant struggle to open my mind to new ideas without judgment, all those memories finally found their place within me.

It is incredible how, as I try to open my mind and my heart to new alternatives, with the intention of giving way to the potential of acquiring new knowledge, my ignorance, instead of diminishing, makes me feel that it takes strength in letting me know that I don't know anything and that I haven't learned what I think I want to learn.

The more that new experiences participate in my life, the greater the feeling of loneliness that is generated in me. I feel that knowledge can be my greatest enemy in my spiritual evolution, and perhaps it can be the greatest obstacle to raise awareness of the divinity in myself and in others. Maybe I already know everything, but I don't know how to express it to be used in my life and in the sharing with others. Perhaps I am much more than I imagine and the divinity is more in me than what religion has instructed me.

After spending several days in Xiahe, we continued our journey northwest along the Yellow River into the desert. The long stretches of land sown with wheat made the first two days literally a golden experience. Witnessing the golden-yellow ears of wheat dancing with the wind was truly magical –a necessary psychotherapy of peace and tranquility. The original plan was to cross the desert to reach Lanzhou, one of the main centers of the Muslim-Chinese population.

As we advanced, the landscape became drier and browner, with a corresponding increase in temperature. The houses were like adobe shoeboxes with tiny windows, much like the ones painted by a child. The front walls were painted white, and wheat fields were spread around the houses. Many people of all ages beat the wheat by throwing it into the air, so that the wind would carry the bran or husk of the wheat grain. Another group of people beat the wheat against the ground with shovels, and another group collected it by sweeping the bran, since they used it daily, mixing it with water as a source of vitamins and fibers, and above all to prevent cholesterol from rising in their blood . Many of them commented, according to what the translator told us, that drinking a glass of water with a tablespoon of wheat bran a day kept them from gaining weight.

On the third day of this journey, heavy rains began to fall, making the road a mud pool. We were entering the part of China that was off-limits to foreigners. Every eight to ten kilometers, there was a checkpoint with a military patrol. Two or three soldiers climbed on the truck to check our passports and the special permission of the government to cross the region, of course, without losing the opportunity to check every corner and every detail of the truck, including our luggage. Already after the second inspection, our belongings were on display. The truck in the back looked like a flea market for clothes and utensils. Some military men were simply indifferent, but others were cruel, inappropriate, rude, and aggressive. The area we were passing through was where the nuclear plants and underground military bases were located. There were only military personnel.

After a few days, we reached the western part of the Great Wall of China – the forbidden part. It was amazing how the Great Wall took five centuries to build – XIII to XVIII. It was built to defend the Chinese territory from nomadic and barbarian invaders from North Asia, as well as from the Mongolian people and the caravans that transported silk from the Middle East to Europe. The route that these caravans took was known as The Silk Road.

The length of the Great Wall was approximately 10,000 kilometers, but almost two-thirds of it was in ruins. It was built with blocks of mud, stones, and straw. Its width at the base was ten meters, and at the top, two meters. The cross section was like that of a truncated pyramid. Every five hundred meters, there was a fifteen-meter-high truncated pyramid-shaped tower with a twenty-meter-wide base, protruding five meters from each side of the Great Wall. Every fifteen kilometers, there was a fortress with a capacity for one thousand soldiers. In each fortress, the walls were reinforced with additional stones and granite, and there were two huge, wooden and iron gates on each side of the fortress, which allowed soldiers to cross from one side of the wall to the other.

We camped on the outskirts of a small town called Jiajuhuan. I spent most of the afternoon and part of the night with the soldiers, trying to share with them, communicate with them and learn from them. They invited me to drink after midnight when they had finished their duties, but unfortunately I had to decline the offer because I was not feeling well. In the last twenty to twenty-four hours, I had had a fever and was dehydrating, both from the fever and from the high local temperature, which was between thirty-eight and forty degrees Celsius in the shade. Added to this, there was my already known difficulty in drinking water which, by the way, was quite hot. Around eight p.m., I walked into my tent, after vomiting twice, as I felt very dizzy and had quite severe back and abdominal pain. I was really afraid; being a doctor made me think about the potential causes. Those possible clinical diagnoses were carrying a roller coaster of conflicting emotions and more fears, when thinking about the potentialities of treatment in that very isolated region of China.

Unfortunately, things got worse in the next few hours. The vomiting became more frequent, with almost no gastric content in them, and the abdominal pain became more and more intense with a tendency to radiate towards the lower right part of the abdomen. I started shaking all over and sweating profusely. In that interim, I took the highest possible doses of pain relievers and antispasmodic medications that I had with me. The abdominal pain became so intense that only a slight movement of my legs increased it. It was raining heavily outside, and the wind was so strong that the tent came loose and part of it became covered with water and mud. Time passed so slowly that the minutes seemed like hours. Meanwhile, my mind kept thinking about all the potential diagnoses. Around eleven p.m., I lost consciousness.

When I woke up again, about thirty to forty minutes later, I found myself in a corner of the tent, sweating and shivering. The pain was almost unbearable. It was located between the lower part of my belly and the right pelvis, with sudden episodes of increase in intensity, with radiation to the genital area and my right leg. I tried to leave the tent to ask for help, even though it was raining heavily, but during the process of getting out, I lost consciousness again. I woke up about two hours later, with my upper body outside the tent in a puddle of mud and water. All I was thinking about was trying to get to the truck to ask the guides for help.

Between the dehydration, the pain, and the side effects of an almost-overdose of pain relievers, I was so confused and disoriented that it took me several minutes to try to get to the truck for help. I got to the truck around three a.m. Almost everyone was inside the truck, because their tents had collapsed in the heavy rain. I remember their faces just before I passed out again. I woke up in the back of the truck, with one of the drivers holding my head and drying my body. From what I remembered, she was saying, "Please don't die, keep breathing... don't die..."

Meanwhile, the truck was speeding towards the nearest populated area. The jumps that the truck hit, due to the bad road conditions, really made me lose control over the pain. While I was in the truck, I was trying to explain, in a few words, what was happening to me, so that the Chinese translator could explain it to the doctors. The pain worsened towards the area of the right kidney, the right groin, and the right leg. The fifty to sixty minutes it took for the truck to get to Jiajuguan, were hours for me.

Upon our arrival at the only medical center in that city, I could not get up by myself, as I was very weak and in a lot of pain. I vomited two more times on the way to the small medical facility. Outside the front door, there was a barefoot doctor smoking in a rocking chair, in his underwear. There were no stretchers or wheelchairs. He asked us to follow him to the second floor, as he wanted to draw blood from me. He put on some plastic flip-flops and started walking in front of us. The two drivers carried me between them. Going up the stairs was not easy, but I finally made it to the second floor and was placed on a high wooden table covered by a green hospital sheet. He drew some blood from me and put in an IV connected with normal saline. I asked him directly, through the translator, to please give me painkillers, but the doctor ignored us, while the Chinese translator told me to be patient.

About three hours later, two doctors in short, white T-shirts and plastic aprons came to the door of the room, where I was to speak to the translator. Later, the translator approached me and told me that he had told the doctors that I was also a doctor and that I wanted to know all the details. The doctors gave him the results of the blood test. In summary, the blood count showed 18,700 white blood cells, ninety percent neutrophils, and twenty-one percent immature cells, which in common parlance meant I had an acute bacterial infection. I told the translator to ask them, in a good way, if they could give me some kind of painkiller. They replied that they couldn't, as they had to wait until the surgical doctor came. At that moment, I understood that they thought I had acute appendicitis, and that is why they could not give me painkillers until the surgical doctor examined me. For the next four to five hours, I fell asleep intermittently for short periods of time.

In the middle of the morning, the surgical doctor arrived. Without saying a word, he began to palpate my abdomen, looking for my painful reaction as he pushed. After less than a minute, he left without saying anything, despite my constant questions through the translator. Outside the room where I was, he spoke with the other two doctors and with the Chinese-English translator. After a couple of minutes, the other two doctors and the translator came up to me. Through the translator, they told me that they needed to open my abdomen to see what was happening. They were going to look through a fluoroscope first, and in five to six hours, the surgical doctor would operate. At that time, my only concern was my pain, and I asked the translator several times to tell them that I needed something for the pain.

The doctors responded in English, "Okay, okay..."

A few minutes later, a nursing assistant, who was spitting on the ground every ten to twenty seconds and was greasy and smelly, gave me two intramuscular injections and connected an intravenous line with a bottle of saline solution and another bottle with glucose solution.

Regardless of how dirty the place was from the mud and the number of flies that accompanied me, I felt somewhat relaxed and calm. It might have been because I wanted to believe that they knew what they were doing.

After half an hour or so, I started to feel better about my pain, but worse about my overall medical condition. I slept for about an hour, until the nursing assistant asked me to get up to go to the X-ray room. I did not understand what he was verbally saying, but his body language made me follow him. It was not easy to get myself off the wooden table and walk, unaided, to the X-ray room which was about ten meters away. The Chinese-English translator had returned with the truck to the camp.

My mind was thinking about this strange life-teaching experience. After studying and working in academic hospitals in the United States, before coming on this adventure, I was now a patient going through this medical torture.

The X-ray room had a very old fluoroscope like the one used fifty or sixty years ago in hospices for patients with pulmonary tuberculosis. Without much delicacy to say, the nurse, without speaking, pushed me to stand behind the fluoroscope screen. He started pulling my pants down, which I helped with, leaving my body naked, with the pants around the ankles. He was pushing me from behind for me to stick to the screen, which was cold and dirty. The three doctors walked in and stood in front of the screen. I could see them, as the screen was up to my neck.

Their clothes were interesting. The three of them wore boxer shorts and white tank tops. They wore plastic flip-flops, and their feet were very dirty, with mud up to the middle of their legs. They started talking to each other for several minutes, and then they pulled up three iron chairs to sit and watch my body on the screen. During all that time, the X-rays passed through my body. They asked me to take a deep breath, to hold the air, etc. As a doctor, I couldn't help but worry at the time about the enormous amount of radiation I was receiving. They had been watching me behind the screen for almost thirty minutes. I was confused and tired.

The pain had lessened. My mind allowed humor and imagination to entertain itself, sending images to my consciousness of thousands of my sperm cells suffering and dying.

After this not very pleasant and even embarrassing experience, a doctor pulled my arm while pointing at my clothes with the finger of the other hand, instructing me, in his unique body language, to get dressed and go back to where I was before. The feelings of returning to my table-bed, walking alone and in pain, led me to experience something that was beyond loneliness, sadness and fear; it was like being in limbo. Nothing was clear, and a passive acceptance was invading my mind, my soul and my being, in an inevitable way.

Later that day, around eight p.m., another surgeon-doctor came to examine me. He was kinder but dirtier, spitting on the floor every minute or two. Every time he cleared his throat for material to spit out, a feeling of nausea would try to make me throw up. Unfortunately the Chinese translator was not there. I had no idea what they were planning to do with me. I knew within me that my diagnosis was between acute appendicitis, or kidney stones somehow stuck between the kidney and the bladder. In the differential diagnosis, acute enteritis and/or cholecystitis could have been involved. I was so weak that thinking about the possible diagnosis was weakening me further, pushing me into a kind of agonizing depression. Perhaps all this was nothing more than pure fear, in all its forms, before the imminent reality that an exploratory surgery of my abdomen was approaching in that rudimentary facility.

A few minutes later, one of the doctors arrived with five different glass syringes. It had been a long time since I had seen those types of syringes. I think they were no longer used since the early 80s. For a few seconds, my mind was invaded by questions about the aseptic measures that were used to sterilize them, but the first needle in my arm produced enough pain to erase those thoughts from my mind, and the other four on my buttocks completed the job. Every time he inserted a needle into my body, I just said, "Xie-xie ni," which was the equivalent of "thank you" in that part of China. After the fifth injection I closed my eyes, trying not to think that my skin had not been cleaned and was very dirty from the rains and mud. The absence of vital signs or temperature measurement since my arrival made the outlook even weirder. A few minutes later, I started to feel better. The pain was starting to decrease in my back and abdomen, and I was falling asleep.

I thought they gave me some pre-anesthetic medications. I prayed with sadness and loneliness that was born from a constant anguish. Really, at that moment, life gave me the opportunity to learn to trust and let what was happening flow, with faith and hope, and that I had not come this far to stay there under those circumstances. I tried to put the best of myself, my family, and the people I loved into my mind, as I struggled not to fall asleep.

I was asleep for several hours. I was awakened by pain in my back and abdomen, accompanied by a headache and chills. The sunlight was already on my face. It was around six a.m. The first thing I did was touch my arms for needles and my abdomen for stitches. What a relief to know that they did nothing. A feeling of gratitude flooded me, that made me cry and laugh at the same time. I felt protected by the divinity, especially in the ways that I had known it the most throughout my life: God, Jesus, and the Virgin Mary.

Around nine in the morning, the surgeons mentioned above came to see me, accompanied by our Chinese-English translator. What a sense of relief it was to see the translator. The doctors began to explain to the translator, and he, with his very limited English, translated for me. Of course, I kept myself abreast of the amount of information that was losing in translation. He was trying to tell me that the doctors thought I had acute appendicitis, complicated by bilateral kidney stones, due to prolonged severe dehydration, and that they needed to do some surgical procedure as soon as possible. After the Chinese-English translator finished explaining to me, the doctors left the room without even looking at me.

Between my fear and anxiety and the translator's poor knowledge of English, who kept repeating to me, "Don't worry, don't worry!, my worries increased exponentially in minutes.

Amid attempts to try to get additional information from the Chinese-English translator about what the doctors were planning to do, the same doctor mentioned above entered the room with three syringes. Without opening his mouth, he pushed me to my left side and injected them into my right buttock without cleaning the skin, just like he did before.

After several minutes the pain improved significantly, and I was flying between fantasies, delusions, and the real world. That pleasant sensation lasted for several minutes and was suddenly interrupted when I saw two of the doctors, mentioned above, arrive in the room with a tray with various needles approximately eight, twelve and sixteen inches long. They looked like the old needles used for amniocentesis – to get amniotic fluid from a pregnant uterus – in the 1950s.

They started pushing me to get me onto my right flank. I got really scared and started saying, "No, no, no," louder and louder, until they stopped what they were trying to do and went looking for the Chinese-English translator.

The translator entered the room, accompanied by one of the expedition's guide-drivers. As soon as I saw them, I asked them why they weren't taking me to the operating room for the surgery they were talking about. The two of them just said that I had to cooperate with them for my own good, and they gave me no other explanation. I sat on that table-bed, and with a fairly severe pain that came from my back towards the genital area, I told the guide that I was very worried and needed to hear the truth of all of this. Seeing my concern and painful discomfort, the driver-guide broke the silence and told me that there was no operating room and that the surgical procedure they were talking about involved inserting those needles into my abdomen. In seconds I understood that I had no alternative, and I asked the translator to tell the doctors to forgive if my attitude was not appropriate and that I was very grateful for their help. I think it was my self-preservation instinct that was trying to create some kind of bond with them.

I accepted this with solidarity, placed my body the way they wanted and closed my eyes. A strong feeling of goodbye, along with sadness that was born from each and every one of my cells in my body, invaded me, making me cry. My tears were sliding down the corners of my closed eyes. Images of my family were flashing through my mind. I tried to stay calm and focus on relaxing. Praying was part of that whole process. It was not easy. After a few minutes, a strange but intense sense of peace took control of my emotions.

In a few minutes, I learned, firsthand, that the art of being a doctor was not about knowledge, but about giving the best of what you have in order to improve or try to improve the quality of health of patients. Like any other patient with pain, fear and uncertainty, I wanted to say to these doctors, "I am in your hands. Please, do the best you can."

In that moment, I realized that this was an expression based entirely on my fear as a patient. All of us doctors did the best we could, at all times, to try to help the patient we were treating. Those doctors were doing the same with me.

My medical restlessness began to stop controlling my thinking and my feeling. In a few minutes, I was incorporated into my condition as a patient and began to let events flow with faith and hope. My subconscious invaded my conscious, leaving it cornered, while making my thinking start to control my emotions again, telling me that I had become a passive patient. My mind, my feelings and my emotions began to create the image in my consciousness of the toad in a pot of water that was heating up little by little, without realizing that they were cooking it and that it is going to die being boiled.

They moved me back to lie on my back and began the surgical procedure. I did not know if it was due to what they gave me in the injections, or due to my resignation and acceptance of the last moments, but I kept looking at those doctors inserting the aforementioned long needles in my abdomen, and on my part there was no reaction. The translator was by my side, telling me what the doctors were doing. The first needle was directed towards my left kidney to try to suck the accumulated urine through the needle. After this explanation, the only thing that came to mind is that maybe life had this in its plans. The fact that they entered my abdomen, without any guidance and only with anatomical knowledge, to do things that did not make sense to me in my limited information on the opinions of allopathic medicine, and that in the criteria of the same are in their essence dangerous and contraindicated, was for me the beginning of the end.

The needles had a stylet inside; this was to protect the end of the needle from cutting me while they are being inserted. When they felt that they were in the area they were looking for, they took out the stylet, and with a glass syringe they aspirated the contents. Every time they aspired and nothing came out, they put the stylet back on the needle and kept inserting it deeper and deeper. My mind was moving to another dimension.

The needles entered on both flanks. One of them, from what I understood, was going to my bladder, and when they inserted a needle into the lower right part of my abdomen to suck out the infection and wash the area by aspirating and injecting saline locally, I thought that I was dying. The pain was excruciating, and my vision was so blurry that I couldn't see the faces of the doctors. I guess I passed out.

About ten hours later, the driver-guide and the anthropologist came to wake me up to tell me that the international insurance I had could not be contacted and that I had to pay the medical expenses out of my pocket. The anthropologist, without any remorse, compassion or pity, told me, without mincing words, that unfortunately they couldn't wait for me. The vehicle-truck was outside the health center, and they were going to pick up the rest of the people from the expedition to leave via Dunhuang, which was approximately six to eight hours from there. He brought my belongings and my passport.

All this caught me totally off guard. I didn't know what to say. It was like I was mentally paralyzed in shock for a few minutes, I didn't know what to say beyond, "It's okay... I understand." He told me that when they came back to Jiajuguan, where I was, they would leave my tent that they had forgotten to bring to me. After they left, an anxious and inevitable crying came over me. I was trying to think what to do. My brain was telling me that if I did not receive antibiotics in high doses and for many days, it is most likely that a severe infection in my abdomen could threaten my life in a few days.

I tried to call my family in Venezuela for almost two hours, but the rudimentary phone system was unable to communicate. Time was running out. I had a decision to make before the truck came through here. If I stayed there, the future would also be quite uncertain, besides not being able to understand a word from them or be understood by them. In my belongings, I had cash in dollars and euros hidden and camouflaged. I paid the medical costs. They gave me the bill on a paper, written in Chinese, with the amount to be paid in dollars. Of course, they took advantage of the circumstances and charged as they pleased. I got dressed and sat on top of my military bag, waiting for them. The pain in my back and abdomen was increasing in intensity very quickly, but my existential worries kept my mind off of it.

Loneliness, depression, frustration, disappointment, fear and uncertainty were playing volleyball, using my next move as a ball in that ambush of my life. After half an hour or so of sitting on top of my bag and trying to think, without really thinking, the driver-guide and the translator arrived. I got up without showing my pain, at least as much as I could, and asked them to call the doctors. Only one doctor came. I asked him if he could provide me with antibiotics and painkillers, because I was going with the expedition. The reaction of the driver and the translator revealed that in their minds they did not want me to continue with them. Upon perceiving that feeling in a fast and forceful way and before they could react, I transformed myself into an angry bear, and everything I said to them became such strong and determined orders that no thought was allowed on their part, nor from anyone on the expedition. No one, apparently, had a clue about this side of me, not even myself.

The doctor told the translator, apparently emphatically, that if I left the health center, I would die. Before he finished his sentences in Chinese, I asked the translator to tell him that I was totally responsible, and I was in total control of me, and that I needed antibiotics and pain relievers. Right after I finished saying that I grabbed my bag and started walking towards the reception of the health center. My determination and anger gave me enough strength to give the impression that I was fine.

The center sold me some pain pills and three injections of intramuscular penicillin that were injected, one in my arm and one in each buttock. The nurse also gave me an injection in my arm of some kind of strong painkiller and told the translator that it was free.

So that no one on the expedition would fear that I was going to continue with them, I walked towards the truck as a soldier. Smiling and waving to everyone in the truck, I went straight to a compartment behind the drivers, where I could lay down. Whatever they injected me with before leaving the health center worked quite well. Even though the truck was jumping, due to poor road conditions, I was able to get to Dunhuang without much mishap.

While I was in the back of the drivers cabin, between sleeping and thinking, I managed between my mind and my heart the differences between using and being used, between being used and the need to belong, between instinct and intention, between naivety and willingness to serve, between believing that you are for what you are and believing that you are because they need you temporarily and circumstantially. Already this trip had landed abruptly in another reality. My mission now was not to try to search for a mission, but to try to survive those new realities until I managed to return to the place where I came from – to return to my family in Venezuela.

As soon as I got off the truck, I took a taxi – a boy on a bicycle pulling a two-wheeled carriage, with capacity for one person – to go to the local health center. Unfortunately, it was significantly worse than the one I was in before, but they were able to sell me antibiotics, pain relievers and whatever else I might need, only if I paid them in German marks. Once again, money turned out to be the universal key.

I bought the strongest intravenous antibiotics they had. I didn't know what kind they were, because everything was written in Chinese and others in Russian. They also sold me ten ampoules of something that was supposed to be morphine, a mercury thermometer, a box of twenty-four vials of 500 cc of 9% saline solution, two IV connections, thirty-six vials of oral protein supplement and two plastic syringes, with their respective needles, from Pakistan. Here I allowed confidence to bloom in me with all its splendor, as I had no other choice. The placebo effect generally improves the patient by seventy to eighty percent. If I kept my mind and all its paraphernalia of acquired knowledge with the closed mouth, whatever it was I had bought, I was already determined to use my placebo effect, hoping that the remaining percentage would be obtained by the basic essences that were in what I was buying, and that they were what they told me they were. At all times, I think I was aware of the loss of information in the limited use of language on both sides. Perhaps they had told me other things about what I was buying, but my mind had already designed the whole script, so that my emotions and my feelings could act without difficulty in the play that was coming.

In a bar, I found cotton bags and two bottles of alcohol smuggled from Pakistan. I rented a room in a motel across from the health center, just in case. I put the small bed in the center of the room and all the supplies around me. I plugged three bottles of intravenous saline into my left forearm, to last for the next ten to twelve hours. I injected twice the highest recommended doses of antibiotics, into the same vein, mixed with the saline, along with one of the morphine ampoules.

I slept for a few hours, but I was awakened by a tremor throughout my body, accompanied by profuse sweating. I had a high fever – 104 degrees F. The pain in my back around the kidney area was increasing with a paroxysmal pattern. I was so weak that it was difficult for me to roll over to get a bottle of the oral solution by the bedside. Just coughing made me vomit. A dense and overwhelming loneliness was what was breathed in that room.

How small the world looked when my health was far from me.

After two days at the motel, I was feeling much better, still with spikes in fever, chills, and a constant, dull ache in my kidneys and lower abdomen. I went back to the health center to buy several portable urinalysis kits and some promised Russian antibiotics. The urine test kits were necessary due to the fact that on the first night in the motel I began to have very dark urine. I prepared myself the best I could to be ready to continue the journey.

The next day, when I was sitting in the truck to go to Kashgar through the desert, the anthropologist told me that they preferred that I not continue with them, because, due to my ailments, I could jeopardize the pre-set program they had. They stayed in Dunhuang to continue later with the other group of guides that they had previously hired. The other two in the group were standing in front of me, not saying a word or saying goodbye. I already knew what I wanted to do. They asked me for the reports that I had up to that moment, and I gave them to them, while thanking them for having given me the opportunity to be part of the expedition and for the quality of the time shared. They lowered their gazes to the ground and walked away.

For my part, I continued to take oral antibiotics and pain relievers during the day. At nights inside the tent, I used intravenous antibiotics. Urine remained positive for blood and protein for the next four days. With the pain reliever I was taking, I was able to control my back pain, but the nausea and vomiting appeared every time I tried to drink or eat something.

We were approaching the desert. The temperature ranged from 105 to 115 degrees F. Sand dust was on us everywhere. We had scarves, caps and special glasses to cover our heads and eyes. Winds and sandstorms kept us from moving at the speed we wanted –only a few tens of kilometers per day. The road we took was parallel to the "Silk Road." This segment became famous between the 7th and 16th centuries, used by Buddhism to spread its doctrine throughout this part of Asia. We camped one night outside the Mogao Caves, also known as "The Caves of the Thousand Buddhas." They were hundreds of square excavations in a great mountain carried out for more than eight hundred years by Buddhist monks. Each of these square excavations had a painting explaining its history, and Buddha statues of different sizes and shapes. About six hundred of these excavations remained intact. Visitors were only allowed to visit twenty of them. In the center of the mountain were two gigantic statues of Buddha, one about thirty-four meters high and the other about twenty-eight meters.

Unfortunately, the Japanese, Russians and English stole much of the statues and wall paintings during the 18th and 19th centuries. With the painkillers I was taking – not knowing what type they were –I knew that they relieved my pain and lowered my fever, in addition to stimulating my perception, since, inside the caves, my imagination seemed to move to different levels of creation, making me travel in time.

The next day we continued the journey through hills of sand, which were formed on a primitive path made of stones. It was the only way to cross that part of the desert. Trying to walk around when the truck was stopping, to meet the relevant physiological needs, was not easy. The surroundings were made up of sand dunes of all sizes, and walking on the smaller ones was difficult, as one sank almost to the knees.

We followed that road towards the city of Turfan, which was located at 154 meters below sea level – the second-deepest depression in the world after the Dead Sea in Jordan. The temperature continued to rise. Inside the truck, in the shade, the temperature varied between 108 and 120 degrees F. Every hour or so, the turbulence of the wind covered us completely with sand. The sand was very hot. The truck was using the windshield wipers to try to see through the sand clouds.

Crossing the Taklimakan Desert, in China's Xinjiang Uygur autonomous region, was a truly hot and dirty experience. Thank God the temperature dropped to freezing levels at night, and that allowed me to rest inside my quite comfortable sleeping bag. It was an adventure trying to keep the tents touching the ground at night. Despite the fact that concrete blocks were placed in each corner of the inside of the tent and a special technique was used to secure the tents, the strong, sandy wind sometimes made me roll over and over inside the tent. Some nights I had the feeling that at any moment the strong wind was going to make me fly through the desert.

The people we found along the way were mainly Chinese-Muslim. The women covered their entire bodies with dark clothing, including their faces. They could see through the veil that covered them. Only married women left an open space on their faces, where the root of the nose and eyes could be seen. They all wore long pants.

The local bread was fabulous and became my "our daily bread." It was the only thing I was capable of eating, plus I really liked it. I could say that the Muslim-Chinese bread from the desert was my delicacy of the gods and my divine sustenance. It was my bread of life. The bread was an oily bread shaped like a pizza, mixed with onion and baked in primitive stone ovens. Those ovens were built in a round shape with stones, leaving a hole in the upper part. A wood fire was made in the center of them, and the pizza dough stuck to the hot inner walls of the oven. The large, round ovens had multiple holes in the walls for air to pass through. In the distance, they looked like weird, giant golf balls.

Two or three times during the day and at night, herds of camels, generally between fifteen and thirty at a time, passed by, leaving behind their characteristic special smell and their respective physiological gifts.

The route was getting faster, mainly when we took "The Yellow Road." This roughly 60-kilometer-long road was built about 180 years ago, to encourage people to pass through the Taklimakan Desert. The yellow bricks were placed to make different figures along the way. It was quite beautiful and surprising to see that road in the middle of hundreds of kilometers of sand dunes and desolation.

A few days later, we reached a small oasis – about two kilometers by five hundred meters. It was not like the oases that movies etch in our minds. This was a composition of dry bushes, millions of mosquitoes, twenty to thirty local herders, hundreds of goats, and dozens of camels. The smell of that oasis was responsible for generating a deep and prolonged memory of that place.

By the way, I almost forgot to explain the meaning of the word "Taklimakan," which means "to enter but not to leave."

Along the way, we found many tombs with the typical characteristics of the area. The graves were mainly piles of sand about two to three meters high. They placed the deceased in the upper part and covered him/her with stones, and in the center of the stones there was a tombstone, where the most outstanding segment of his/her life was written. The writing on the tombstone looked in the direction of Mecca.

At the top, on the sides of the tombstone, were crows carved from wooden logs. Important people were mummified and placed in a small cave at the base of the sand mountain. There were no restrictions on visiting the graves. The mummies in many tombs were very well preserved in that environment, after thousands of years.

On two occasions, in the areas close to where we camped at night, we found the corpses of two men who were cut in half at the waist. One half of the corpse was placed with the head facing east, and the other half with the feet facing west. Based on the information obtained through the translator, apparently people who committed a crime in the community were sentenced to death by cutting them in half. They would place their halves apart for their spirits to roam the desert for all eternity.

Coming from 1,800 meters above sea level to 154 meters below sea level was not easy. My body had lost the ability to adapt to what the circumstances deserved. About two hundred kilometers from Turpan, an oasis began to open up in the middle of the desert, with a river in the center trying to carve its way, leaving a gorge that was getting deeper and deeper as the river descended. The walls of the gorge were formed by very dry, reddish rocks, with the scars of years of erosion that gave the sensation, combined with the extremely hot temperature, of looking at hell itself. It was no wonder that it was called "The Flaming Mountains."

Before arriving in Turpan, we had the opportunity to stay for a few days in the ancient city of Jiaohe. We enjoyed the vineyards on both sides of the river, as well as the locomotives of the steam trains of this part of China, which pulled dozens of old, wooden wagons that went to and from Turpan. This city was magical. It was a true oasis, in the middle of an inhospitable desert.

Upon our arrival in Turfan, its unique nature gave us a real, warm welcome. We arrived at around ten p.m., and the local temperature was 115 degrees F. For those who are using degrees Centigrade or Celsius, the temperature was forty-five to forty-six degrees.

Turfan was quite a peculiar city. Its surface was very arid, but within it dozens of underground rivers and streams made their way. It had a unique pumping system. The water was brought to the surface, where it ran in thin open channels through the vineyards, trees and streets. The water was pumped with great force every day between three p.m. and five p.m. During that period of time, the local population bathed and washed clothes. They bathed in clothes in the open air and used the soap under their clothes. It was a true water festival.

Participating in that water festival, the days we spent in the city not only made me feel much better physically, but also emotionally and existentially.

To prevent the evaporation of the water, the water ran through handmade underground channels, built between the 7th and 10th centuries. Those channels were located between three and eight meters below the surface, and there were more than 3,000 thousand kilometers of channels below the city. In the center of the city, there were underground roads on the sides of the canals for the mobilization of people. It was a super effective and functional underground walking transport system." Hundreds of people were walking in it.

The temperature in the underground channels was between sixty and seventy degrees F during the day. On the ceiling and the walls of those channels, you could see the roots of the trees on the surface. The water came from deep underground rivers that originated in the mountains, hundreds of kilometers away. Deep perforations made by hand allowed the water to be brought to the surface for the irrigation of their crops. That irrigation system was called "Karez."

The visit to the ancient tombs of Astana and the Jiaohe Ancient City built four thousand years ago allowed me to glimpse new aspects of the true nature of human life and, mainly, to have a better understanding of the population of Chinese living in that zone. When I was trying to mix with them, I could appreciate, in the vast majority, a special look in their eyes that radiated wisdom.

On several occasions, I would simply sit in front of a group of older people, without trying to say a word or make any kind of movement. I just remained looking at them, observing and learning. In a strange way, after about half an hour of looking at them, I was beginning to feel a very unique connection to their ancestral universe. It was like sleeping awake, not feeling my body and not knowing where my mind and thoughts were. It was like transporting me to "no man's land." Time was passing so quickly that I could sit and watch them for hours without feeling any kind of physical fatigue.

Walking through the ruins of Jiaohe Ancient City, I was surprised to see how many Buddha statues were worshiped by the people who lived there. For example, there was a temple located in the center of the city with 101 statues of Buddha, and around it were twenty-five other small temples, all of them with their own statue of Buddha.

Due to the reddish rocks through which rivers and streams passed, the water was brown, and due to the high temperature it had, you had to take a sip and keep it in your mouth for several seconds before swallowing it. Otherwise each sip of water could not only cause nausea, but also induce vomiting.

After a few days, we continued our journey to the rural community of Hotan. Here I had the great opportunity to share very closely with the local people. They allowed me to enter their houses, and with body language and a mixture of words in Chinese, English, Portuguese and French, we shared thoughts and emotions in our own way in a kind of spiritual conversation.

Many of the locals had rudimentary silk factories in their homes. The silkworms, inside their white cocoons and still alive, floated and jumped in large pots filled with hot water, producing filaments of silk. All the workers were women. With their left hand they were collecting the silk filaments that the worms produced in the pots, and with their right hand they held the silk filaments to a thin wire. Another woman seated on the right side was taking the silk filaments from the wire to attach them to a wooden mill wheel moved by pedaling with her foot. She was winding the silk thread on a wooden reel. The houses inside had a fairly small space for all those people and all the paraphernalia involved. The heat inside was incredibly intense. That, accompanied by the strange, strong and penetrating odors, plus thousands of flies, were generating a saturated atmosphere in which it was difficult to breathe.

The silk thread was almost transparent. Another group of women were in charge of dyeing the spools of silk thread with different colors. Those reels were unwrapped again to be rewound onto much larger reels. Those big reels were the ones that were sold to factories.

There were many small home factories around, where women sat in front of long, wooden spinning wheels, while moving six pedals with their feet at a fascinating pace, weaving and spinning the silk threads of different colors to make beautiful silk fabrics.

In the same town, I was able to see and enjoy the local people who worked in the home carpet factories. Almost all the workers were also women. They were laughing and talking to each other, probably about me, but we had fun together. Amid the laughter and talking, at no time did they stop mixing the threads in the manufacture of rugs. Many of those rugs were several meters wide and many more meters long.

That Muslim Chinese population had two peculiar customs in their eating habits, that they insisted on sharing with me. One of them was to eat their specialty –the devouring bee bird. That plate consisted of a dozen tiny fried birds of approximately eight by four centimeters each, which were called devouring bees. They take the birds out of a cage where there were hundreds of them, and they throw them alive in a large saucepan with boiling oil, which, from a distance, looked almost black. After a minute or two, they were removed and placed on a metal tray, ready to eat. The custom was to eat them hot, burning the tips of the fingers. First, their necks were broken, their heads pulled off the body, then both legs ripped off.

What was left to eat was a three-and-a half-centimeter-by-two-centimeter chunk of hot, oily, fried poultry meat.

To be honest, the first four or five of them that I ate, I swallowed without even touching them with my teeth, giving them a hypocritical smile and pretending that I was enjoying it. Then I decided to be more honest and started eating them by taking small bites and savoring the meat. The truth is that I liked them, and my displays of satisfaction and appreciation changed to more complex facial expressions, vocal sounds and smiles with authentic expression. The meat tasted like a mixture of chicken and frog legs in oil broth.

The other specialty was a bit more grotesque and more difficult to eat. It was boiled sheep's head. I tried to eat some meat between its eyes and nose, with great effort. The truth was that it was not very tasty for me. That night I had nightmares, where the body of that sheep looked for its head, and the head screamed and asked for help inside my stomach. The image of that head staring at me as I tried to eat it stayed in my mind for a long time, regardless of whether I was awake or asleep.

After three days, we continued our journey to the northwest, towards the city of Kashgar. Muslim influence was significantly stronger in that area. People there were more contaminated by Western capitalism. There was more aggressiveness and less spirituality. In that area, business, money and technology were displacing customs, traditions and ancient spiritual wisdom at great speed.

All the women were completely covered in clothing. Some of them were wearing sunglasses over their facial veils. They resembled Cousin Itt from the Addams family. The men wore typical hats, and almost all of them had dark beards. Women were really secondary human beings in that Muslim-based society. Many times they gave the appearance of even being abused and mistreated.

Kashgar was a big, old, boring city, not very pretty to say, and had turned into a big market where everything was sold except people. I had never seen so many donkeys together as I had seen in that city.

After spending a few days with local people, visiting schools and hospitals as well as government institutions for the population of people with disabilities, we continued the journey. This time we were heading towards the north of Pakistan on the Karakorum highway.

Sitting in the back of the gigantic vehicle-truck, on that narrow road through the mountains, awakened in me all kinds of phobias of heights, which apparently my mind and my heart had kept hidden for a long time. We spent two days camping at about 3,700 meters above sea level, to adapt to the altitude and cold. Those days were very windy, with temperatures close to zero degrees Celsius. The snow-capped mountains were very dry, and many of their peaks were hidden in a hazy sky.

Our tents were around a small lake, but the winds and cold did not allow us to enjoy the scenery much. While we were going uphill, we crossed several desert plains from where the view of the mountains of 7,000 meters high or more, with their icy peaks and their chromatic reflections of the sunlight, were making me ramble through the ancestral mysteries of those mountains.

It took us several days to reach the Khunjerab Pass – the border between China and Pakistan – at 5,004 meters above sea level. The sight of K-2 – the second-highest mountain in the world, at 8,660 meters – going towards the Pamir mountain range between Pakistan and China, as well as going towards Kailash Mountain, was simply majestic, difficult to describe in words. It was a unique spiritual experience.

Sleeping at night at that height in the tents was quite difficult, in addition to being very cold. Perspiration was forming a thin layer of ice inside the tent. Inside the sleeping bag, it was wet. The temperature at night was staying between -7 and -15 degrees Celsius, but the wind chill factor made it even colder. The longest and worst night was when we were camping at Lake Karakul.

In that area the sunsets were magical, beautiful and with a unique game of colors. The turquoise blue and light-green color of the water was contrasting with the green of the surrounding fields such as golf courses with large gray stones, sheep, camels and yaks scattered towards the lower slopes of the icy and snowy mountains, allowing the sun to reflect in a multicolored gamma that varied as it painted scenes that made me feel like God. The squirrels that played in that area were really huge and fat, almost twice the size of the ones seen elsewhere.

I had the great opportunity to share with several Hindu monks who had been living all their lives along the Hunza River in the mountains. They were fascinating to watch. There was so much peace and natural wisdom in their eyes that I felt mesmerized in their presence.

Speaking in English with them was already a unique kind of blessing. It expressed a part of me that had been imprisoned in my feelings for several months. For days I was with them, asking about so many things: things in life, things about their idea of life, things about their adaptability, things related to loneliness and spirituality, things related to God, the divinity of the creation, more advanced civilizations in contact with us, parallel worlds, etc.

They were fascinating days. I think we all enjoyed ourselves a lot, between questions and answers. One of those days, we went together to visit the Ultar Sar at 6,750 meters above sea level. On the way, so that I could adapt to the altitude, we stopped many times to rest, to do breathing exercises and to observe the surroundings. They saw details that I could not see until after they were explained to me. In the magic of the magnificent scenery, some of them went into deep meditations. Knowing me, they did not waiting for me to ask them, and they told me on their own initiative what they had experienced during their meditations. Their explanations made me open my mind, my feelings and my emotions to different dimensions in relation to the perception of people, of nature, of the interpretation of the universe and of the different ways of coming into contact with God.

We sat gazing at the Ultar Sar for hours. Unfortunately, hours, for me, were not as long as theirs. I was not able to perceive all the sensations consciously during all that time. Perhaps many of the sensations were perceived by my unconscious – I hope so – since I fell asleep for a good while.

While we were returning from the glacier, a family who lived in a small town called Aliabad, about two hours from where we were, arrived accompanied by the local police. As we watched them approach, the monks, almost in chorus, asked me if I was in trouble with the authorities. My spontaneous and sincere response was that I didn't think so. When they arrived at our side, they politely explained that they were there to ask me the favor of going to see their young son who had neurological problems. Everyone in the family and the two policemen who came with them spoke English quite well.

Of course my response was positive and full of thanks for having contacted me with the idea that I could help them. They went down first, since the vehicle with which they had come was parked a bit far away. While we were going down to where they were going to pick me up, between jokes and laughter we were talking about how in China they communicated telepathically, since we did not understand, neither they nor I, how they could have known that I was a neurologist. When we got to the police vehicle, they told us that they had known for several weeks that a neurologist was heading towards his village. And I thought I was passing through China almost unnoticed.

They took me to a nice house hidden in the woods on Batlit Mountain. After examining the nice little boy, named Shenfo, with hemiplegic cerebral palsy, named I stayed talking to them until I saw peace on their faces regarding their son's neurological problem. Trying to thank me, they offered me, every fifteen to twenty minutes, a cup of tea, and pieces of bread and butter on a separate plate. My biggest reward was when I was on my way to the police vehicle to be taken back to camp. The boy's mother came running and hugged me tightly. She was short, so the hug was around my abdomen. In the police vehicle, they explained to me that women were prohibited from expressing emotions to people other than their family. That was a very nice gesture from the whole family, including dad and grandparents. ShenFo was the only son and the only grandson.

As the police dropped me off outside the camp, I was overcome by an uncontrollable desire to cry, mixed with a pleasant sense of satisfaction. Throughout my career as a doctor, in circumstances like this I was not always emotionally ready to hear what I was saying. What I spoke to the relatives was mainly about the love of parents and grandparents; about ShenFo's love, joy, happiness and satisfaction of being and of belonging; about family wisdom; about the divinity involved in the total commitment to the professed love; on the feelings, thoughts and emotions involved in the processes of acceptance of the realities different from those expected; on how to work on improving the perception of the elements that make up our realities; about the unexpected little miracles of life, etc.

Of course, we spoke of the organic brain conditions responsible for the clinical-neurological picture of ShenFo, of alternatives for physical, occupational, emotional, vocational and spiritual therapies.

At dawn the next day, we continued our journey down the narrow road of the Pamir Mountains towards Pakistan, a new cultural experience looming on the horizon. There were blue rivers and glaciers and an overwhelming majority of men on the road, in typical Pakistani clothing –long white, gray, green or brown shirts and light or dark hats – constantly talking and making noises. The trucks and buses were decorated with motifs of all kinds, worked in wood and mixed with mirrors, lights, curtains, multi-colored fabrics, garlands, etc. Everywhere, and twenty-four hours a day, local music was playing at full volume. Occasionally a woman could be seen, covered from head to toe, including her face, in typical clothing. I think one woman appeared on the streets for every 400 to 500 men.

Before reaching Gilgit, a significant number of soldiers were the ones that were forming the scene around us. In that part of northern Pakistan, there were many local political struggles in the form of battles between guerrillas of different stripes. Weapons, rifles and machine guns were the only bush in that desert area, where rocks and dust were the other two elements of nature.

On our way to southwest Pakistan, we spent a few days in the region where the Gilgit and Indus rivers meet the three highest mountain ranges in the world – the Karakorum, the Himalayas and the Indus Kush. Thanks to the clear day, we were able to enjoy the Nanga Parbat peak – the third highest at 8,126 meters. It was seen standing out in a clear, blue sky.

It took us two more days to see K-2. The road was very difficult, but on the second day it was a beautiful day, and the blue sky was without clouds. On that clear morning, the K-2 peak could be seen in its magnitude, light brown and snowy. Like an imposing and gigantic temple, the K-2 stood in the middle of a clear and brilliant, blue sky. It was truly a visual experience that took my breath away.

We continued our journey to Islamabad. The thunderstorms were so strong and frequent that we stayed for a few days in a small town called Besham. People there were very friendly. I had the opportunity to visit several homes and examine several elderly people, mainly with dementia and arthritis. Their houses had a peculiar, sweet smell. It was fascinating to be able to communicate with people in a common language. I was able to obtain from them immeasurably more information, and I felt that I could share with them more of my thinking, my feeling, and my medical experience.

Unfortunately, I had the slow and painful process of passing kidney stones in this town, for the first time in my life. Each movement of those pebbles stole the best of me, and sometimes they would bend me until I fell on the ground. My treatment was to drink as much liquid as possible, with lemon juice. The aforementioned pebbles took their time to surface.

A couple of days later we reached Rawalpindi, the old part of Islamabad. I went straight to a small hospital emergency room. They gave me intravenous pain relievers and told me it was better to go to Islamabad International Hospital. The next morning, I was in the emergency room of the International Hospital –a very good hospital with all high-quality services. Three doctors participated in my evaluations. After six to eight hours, I was informed that, according to the tests results, I needed to be hospitalized, as they had found multiple abnormalities in kidney-function tests, evidence of active infection, and evidence of active inflammation and infection around the appendix and the ascending colon. They did not give me more than the minimum necessary information.

The inability to pay the required deposit in cash, as is customary for poor patients, was the key to getting me back on the street the same day.

I was quite tired, not only physically but also emotionally. Since I started this new adventure in my life several months ago, I had lost around seventy to eighty pounds of weight. Gray hair had taken over from the hair that was struggling to stick to my scalp. At the motel I was staying at in Islamabad, there were mirrors in the bathroom, something that was conspicuous by its absence in my life for many months. My physical appearance had changed significantly. I was worried about the reaction that my family would have when they came to pick me up at the Maiquetía airport in Venezuela in a few days.

In the days of waiting for the logistics to unfold for my return to Caracas – via Karachi-Abu Dhabi-London-Maiquetía – mixed feelings ran through the corners of my mind. There was a mixture of strange frustration, emotional and physical fatigue, as well as uncertainties that did not allow themselves to be defined.

Despite having tried to heal myself physically with the allopathic alternatives, to the extent of the limited possibilities, I really did not believe that the supposed medications were involved in the process. Some of them helped me manage the pain, from moment to moment. I say "supposed," because in reality I do not know if I was really using the antibiotics that they had told me, since they were written in languages that I did not know and did not indicate the doses of them.

Actually, I believe that they acted by producing a placebo effect for my mind, while the wisdom and the consciousness of my body took the initiative to heal me, using my accumulated information in my DNA, in accordance with its connections with each and every one of the cells of my body. I think my body was inspired by the Swiss motto used by The Three Musketeers: Unus pro omnibus, omnes pro uno – one for all and all for one.

I really believe that chemistry did not play any major role, and all healing was at an energy level. Energies that were in me, but that for now, were not at the level of my consciousness.

On the flight to Caracas, I decided to trust what my instincts were making me perceive. That is why, since then, I had not undergone any type of diagnostic procedure based on the extraordinary alternatives that allopathic medicine offered.

The arrival in Caracas was very special for my wife and my six-year-old son, and, of course, for me too. There was a happy expression on their faces, and there was a beautiful illumination in their eyes. In the midst of that family joy, they could not hide their astonishment at seeing me. I think that for them, confronting in their minds and hearts the images they had of me before my departure, with the images they were seeing, was not very easy. Despite all that, the tears of the six eyes did not stop manifesting themselves in their very sui generis idiosyncrasies. I had lost their physical images in my mind, and at first glance they seemed different to me. But their images in my heart had not stopped growing exponentially, allowing me to see them with so much love, that I did not pay attention to what my eyes were seeing.

My son was looking at me all over, as if he was seeing his dad for the first time. My wife proved to be much more special than I ever imagined. Our love for each other grew exponentially in the distance. The three of us were already an equilateral triangle. Since then, it did not matter which side of the triangle stipulated the steps of our lives. We maintained a growing family love, a happiness that spread to our surroundings, and a stability that did not allow itself to be influenced by the ups and downs of live.

The events of this missionary adventure were so varied, so different, so strange, so full of thoughts-and-feeling-conflicting emotions, so human and so divine, that there might not have been words, or that there were all the words, to describe the learnings from my experiences. I only knew that my energies and my frequencies had very varied intensities and wavelengths, making me feel that life was a constant change, that it did not allow us to be what we were, because being what we were did not leave time or space for anything more.

Africa - Zambia

Since my last missionary adventure, I have been, along with the other sides of the equilateral triangle, enjoying as a family what love and respect for our individualities and idiosyncrasies have allowed us to experience. Happiness, joy, enthusiasm, faith and hope have been intermingled with the uncertainties of existential, professional and economic struggles with the passing of the years.

The socioeconomic situation in Venezuela had been deteriorating exponentially, without compassion or truce. Moral standards and cultural tradition, unfortunately and in a way difficult to explain, added to this deterioration. Society as such, adopted the "money god" as the only advisor in its evolution. Life ceased to be life and became survival. Obtaining money at any cost, regardless of the risks involved or the damages to third parties, decapitated the educational and professional leaderships learned and acquired meritoriously. Diplomas lost their value against the dollar. Merits were now based on accumulated dollars. Vanity boasts and vainglory in the power of the purchased dollars. Community action degenerated into, "How much is there for me?"

As a family, we were progressing through that jungle of selfish individualities, maintaining the values that we felt were illuminating our north to follow: benevolence, compassion, love for nature, and respect for the diversity of idiosyncrasies, ideas and religion.

From moments to moments, I had the opportunity to get involved with people with medical needs, who were living in suburban areas, with very low hygienic, existential and economic resources. Those people lived in very precarious places, known in Venezuela as "los ranchos" –similar to the shantytown or favelas of Brazil. Those ranchos were distributed in different communities in the foothills of the mountains that surrounded the city of Caracas. Unfortunately, kind and decent people shared their residential space with antisocial people, sociopaths, and drug addicts, most of them wanted by the police for drug trafficking, robbery, and murder.

The almost imperative need to have political influences, in order to obtain positions for general practitioners and specialists in universities and public hospitals, added to the lack of the economic power necessary to participate in the purchase of shares, an essential requirement, to be part of the medical staff of a hospital or private clinic. They were leaving me plunged in a persistent inability to work in any field related to my professional medical experience. At the same time, the Venezuelan population was experiencing a progressive and uncontrollable spread of HIV infection, increasing the number of AIDS cases every day, with its consequent neurological complications.

Faced with those realities, my family and I made the decision that I return to the United States to study and work in the field of neurological complications associated with HIV and AIDS, which was one of the areas of neurology that I knew the least about.

In mid-1998, I went to New York to do a post-doctoral fellowship in the area of neurological complications, associated with HIV infection and AIDS, in the Neurology Department of the Mount Sinai Medical Center in Manhattan. My tutor and teacher was someone extraordinary, with a professional level of knowledge in the area, who in addition to constantly winning my admiration, stimulated me in my learning, in dimensions that neither he nor I imagined at the time.

Working with the HIV-positive and AIDS population gave me a kind of wisdom to see and feel the lives and struggles of those people, as well as to understand that the battles they had to fight day by day were not because they were necessarily thinking that they were going to win them, but they had to fight them, not only because they were part of their lives, but because they were the seeds they were planting for their future.

This was the first time, of the many that I had been in the United States, that speaking Spanish acquired such an important and necessary role, not only to provide information to the Spanish-speaking community through publications, but also to reach them directly, to share their feelings and their fears, and on many occasions to try to be light, strength and future in their despairs.

Living in the heart of Manhattan allowed me to walk up and down almost daily, observing people and their behaviors. For me, it was an intense training in Behavioral Sciences and Psychopathology. I felt that the famous phrase: "What you see in New York, you probably won't see anywhere else," was almost entirely true. The potpourri of cultures, customs, nationalities, races, lifestyles and distribution of wealth were painting daily a new mural, with its unique singularity that made it very different from the previous ones.

After a year, the family roots and the idealization of my native land pushed me again to return to Caracas, with the illusory illusion that this time things were going to be different. Unfortunately, not only was I very wrong, but things were even worse. After many months of repeatedly experiencing, "No," and "Sorry, but no," in my daily job search or of some way to obtain a stable income to provide my family with the basic needs, my family and I decided to move to Canada, with the idea in our minds of emigrating to that beautiful country.

In the late fall of 1999, we were already living in the province of Manitoba, in the beautiful little town of Brandon, where people made us feel part of them from the beginning. It was for us like an oasis in the desert of our existential turbulence. That was not a desert like the ones I had seen before. That desert stayed all day and all night, with temperatures below zero degrees Celsius, and the meadows were white; not exactly white sand, but snow and ice.

Unfortunately, being Venezuelan and being only certified in my specialty by the American Board of Neurology and Psychiatry of the United States, limited our stay in Brandon. Paradoxically, the Canadian Royal College of Physicians did not allow any doctor trained in the United States and certified by the American Board of the specialty to take the Canadian Board of the specialty if more than seven years had passed since the last year of specialty residency, even though the specialist has been working daily in academic teaching hospitals and/or in private practice since then. In my case, it had been eight years since my last year of residency in neurology. The year, as a postdoctoral fellowship at the Department of Neurology at Mount Sinai Medical Center in New York, was not accepted by the commission that reviewed my appeal.

Because of that, we were only able to stay in Canada for two years, which was the maximum time allowed. During the last year in Canada, we applied for a job in the United States, knowing that I was qualified to obtain the type of O-1 visa.

In July 2001, my family and I arrived in Jacksonville, Florida, with an O-1 visa and a sense of calm and peace of mind, knowing that we could settle down once and for all. I began working in academic and private practice in both pediatric neurology and adult neurology, with the opportunity to teach.

Everything was meshing up fabulously for all of us as a family. Months later, the tragic terrorist attack of September 11 also touched our lives. The O-1 visas were suspended for National Security reasons. This type of visa was also awarded to highly qualified researchers who were working in chemical and microbiology research laboratories in the United States, with potential skills to develop weapons of mass destruction.

They gave us several months to gather our things, in order to return to our countries of origin, and from there to apply for visas for the United States again. My family and I had the opportunity to meet and listen to the tragedies of many other families who had come to the United States with an O-1 visa, and who had already been established for decades in different cities throughout the country. There was no consideration or compassion for those families that were being forced to return to their countries of origin, where they no longer had relatives in them or knew anyone. In several of these countries, the socio-political conditions had changed so much, that if they returned, they would feel like foreigners who had just arrived in an inhospitable country, which was the country where they were born.

We returned to Caracas, with the good luck that we managed to get a good school for our son Ricardo. My wife Carolina immediately started looking for work alternatives. Several months before our departure from the United States, the Department of Epidemiology of the University of Michigan and the World Federation of

Neurology had developed a project to implement an epidemiological training and education program in the area of neurology, in Lusaka, Zambia. The project became known as "Project Zambia." I was invited to start the first phase of the project.

A few weeks after arriving in Caracas and after we had stabilized as best we could, I left on my third missionary expedition. This time, everything seemed very well organized, at least from a distance, and based on e-mail and telephone communications with the University of Michigan and the World Federation of Neurology, who, in turn, were communicating with the School of Medicine of the University of Lusaka, the University of Chainama and the local hospital for Health Sciences.

They explained to me that I was going to be the pioneer of their Zambia project, organized with the aim of creating and establishing, in that part of Africa, the necessary steps towards the structuration of the specialty of neurology, which was very necessary in that region of Africa.

My commitment was to study and analyze the conditions in which the medical communities found themselves and their extension to the population, evaluate the alternatives to train medical and paramedical personnel in the neurological clinical-symptomatic diagnosis, and the potential options for the treatment of the conditions found. The project also included developing and implementing instructional programs for local students, allowing them to use neurology knowledge in the general population. The main idea was to create neurology technicians with the capacities to diagnose, manage and treat neurological patients at the level of a nurse practitioner, in the specialty of neurology.

The idea and the intention were fabulous. I could say that, for me, it was like a chocolate cake with vanilla ice cream on top and a layer of sweetened condensed milk covering it – that is, it is impossible to refuse the temptation. The only thing that was jumping between my instincts with a certain anxious restlessness, was the idea of being the pioneer. But I tried to just think about the potential benefit it could offer and to enjoy the idea that I was going to do what I liked, with everything already organized around me.

I flew to Lusaka, Zambia, with stops in Sao Paulo, Brazil and Johannesburg, South Africa. It was quite a long journey, due to the length of the respective stopovers. Upon my arrival at Lusaka airport, I experienced the first ups and downs. There was no one waiting for me at the airport, as I had been told. The only thing I had was the name of an employee of the Chainama Medical Health Educational Community, who was supposed to be in charge of me for the next few months. They told me how to get to the center, and a spontaneous taxi driver offered me a ride for a certain amount of dollars.

Upon arrival at the facilities of the Chainama Medical Health Educational Community, I realized that no one knew about me. It was already close to seven p.m., and the guard helped me to locate the lady who was supposedly in charge of me, by phone. After an hour, the lady arrived. She was a little surprised and not in a very good mood. She took me to her office and told me that there was only a fax she had received several weeks before, explaining what the project was about, my name and my probable date of arrival in Lusaka, which had not been specified since then. She insisted that I read the fax for myself, but I tried to calm things down. I told her that everything was fine and that, please, to tell me where my accommodation was, and that the next morning we would clarify the details with the authorities in charge. I temporarily stayed in an office, as she didn't know where I should be.

The next morning I met many people, all very friendly, but, as usual, in any project created remotely, there was only an idea and a fax. Already after a few hours, I began to understand a little about the mentality of those people. It was my first experience in Africa.

The Chainama Medical Health Education Community in Lusaka consisted mainly of classrooms for four levels of students, student dormitories and a psychiatric hospital. The constructions were very simple, made with cement bricks, and roofs made with sheets of zinc and/or asbestos. People, in general, had a smile on their faces but were distant and very calm.

As soon as I arrived, I began to contact the different missionary communities in South and Central Africa. I began to get involved with the local educational and medical communities, as well as with the general population, mainly walking around.

There was the need and there was the desire, but the initiative was lost in the uncertainty. Getting started was not easy. I did not know if it was due to the natural idiosyncrasy of the people of Africa who lived in the area, or if it was due to an apathy towards innovation, or if it was the consequence of a habit of staying in the monotony "of the same."

As days went by, I realized that the silent responses to my ideas, to the evaluations and to the diagnosis of the realities that were arising the need to propose alternatives and develop plans to shape the program, hid a strong cultural root of fighting against any attempt to change things. There was a general tendency to avoid knowing that there might be another way of doing things.

By the second week, I was already managing to keep myself as low-key as possible, while I was dropping ideas, making them feel that the ideas came from themselves. A few weeks later, there was great enthusiasm and an inevitable competition among themselves to take ownership of the advances they had made and to enjoy them in the world of their own vanities.

Everything was holding itself between threads but gradually moving towards action and execution. The balance between the components was the cornerstone that allowed me to advance in the development of the project, designed based on the needs and possibilities. The university and government authorities showed an evasion and distancing not easy to understand, at the beginning. I was very new to Africa, but I was already beginning to experience what I called "the law of the lion." Each authority marked their territory and defended it with jealousy and with the use of their power. Sometimes I felt like I was in the middle of the jungle. There were certain specimens in positions of power who seemed to enjoy lifting the leg and splashing me.

The students and medical health personnel, on the contrary, were more enthusiastic to learn and to open their minds to new alternatives, without being afraid to discover the distance between where they were and where they could be.

The British not only left them the English language, but also the slow and complicated old bureaucracy. Paperwork, agendas, memos and committees to study new issues that nobody wants to make decisions about were daily and repetitive obstacles. The cultural and environmental impact took a lot of my energy the first few weeks.

Students, teachers, authorities, and medical staff spoke mainly in English. But the rest spoke their native dialects –Bemba and Nyanja, mainly. Body language was my main form of communication. During the time I spent in Lusaka, I spoke English in the Italian style – that is, making some movement with any part of my body, with each word I said.

Regardless of what they were speaking in English, there was an important gap between what they expressed and what they understood.

Zambians were smiling most of time. They were very conservative, and a lot of them were very religious. They usually met in small groups under a tree or around their houses, to read the Bible, on a daily basis. The ancient wisdom of Africa was floating in the air and somehow flowed in and out of me as I breathed.

Zambia was mainly dry and hot, with great poverty and a "super fly population" that was perceived everywhere. Only to the south, towards Victoria Falls, the environment was much more pleasant, probably due to its tourist importance and English local influence in the past.

Zambia became independent in 1964. By then it had wealth greater than that of its neighbors. It knew its natural resources and had the means to export them. They were mainly copper mines and, to a lesser extent, other materials. There was also no shortage of fresh water, thanks to its large rivers and lakes, so agriculture was reasonably developed. With the progressive closure of the copper mines, Western investment dropped significantly. In the fields, corn production was exponentially reduced, generating poverty in the surroundings. Government mismanagement, embezzlement and corruption opened the doors that led Zambia to its current situation. The AIDS epidemic, progressive poverty, malaria and inclement drought were the major aggravations in the last decade before my arrival.

Zambia became independent in 1964. By then it had wealth greater than that of its neighbors. It knew its natural resources and had the means to export them. They were mainly copper mines and, to a lesser extent, cement and vegetable oils. There was also no shortage of fresh water, thanks to its large rivers and lakes, so agriculture was reasonably developed. With the progressive closure of the copper mines, Western investment dropped significantly. In the fields, corn production was exponentially reduced, generating poverty in the surroundings. Government mismanagement, embezzlement and corruption opened the doors that led Zambia to its current situation. The AIDS epidemic, progressive poverty, malaria and inclement drought had been the great aggravations in the last decade before my arrival.

Going into very poor households, with so many family members with advanced AIDS and/or Falciparum malaria, allowed me to see the other side of the economic globalization. The exploitation of copper kept Zambia as "the African Switzerland" for many years, but the new global economic changes pushed to buy the copper from Chile, leaving this country to die, little by little, without mercy. Thanks to international support, where Japan was playing an important role, Zambia was recovering, at least in the reconstruction of roads and means of transport. Like many countries in socio-economic crisis, the armed army took to the streets and was stationed everywhere.

Several hours a day, I visited families with members who had been diagnosed with AIDS and/or malaria, or who had neurological problems. As part of the intention of gratitude, an invitation to eat was an unavoidable gesture of courtesy. I practically had them two to three times a week. The common denominator was all of us sitting on the floor, sharing together, not only the family members who lived in that house, but also dozens of neighbors. How they enjoyed staring at me and laughing at me and with me. A hot, white dough called "Nshima" with bean broth served on metal plates was the special dish that was offered to me every time I was invited, regardless of the area, the hygiene conditions or the precariousness or not of the houses.

In each house, they explained to me how to eat it. Mainly, it was about taking a portion of Nshima with your left hand, then trying to make a ball with it while moving it between your fingers. Then you dipped the Nshima ball in the bean broth, which was placed in a metal pan to be shared by all.

Don't think it was as easy as I just explained. Every time I took a piece of Nshima, it burned the tips of my fingers and the palm of my hand. Inevitable expressions in Spanish, learned throughout my life, were coming out of my mouth like a reflection. Those expressions or bad words not only were helping me to alleviate the pain a bit, but also made everyone laugh at me, making the moment more pleasant and fun. They told not to worry, and that in a few weeks I would no longer have sensitivity to pain in my fingers, and that I would eat the Nshima without using my Spanish language.

Although I kept my sense of humor afloat at all times, it was not so easy to be surrounded by people who spoke native dialects that you do not understand and stared at you with distance and constant observation. There was something about those people that inspired me to feel calm and secure, as I was walking through suburbs where extreme poverty was manifested everywhere.

Unfortunately, I needed to open doors by tipping in the local currency "kwacha" or in dollars.

Soccer was the national sport. Any round object was used as a ball, and dozens of children and adults played simultaneously. Being a soccer player during my childhood and adolescence helped a lot to open doors with local communities. After not playing soccer for more than 20 years, it became my main tool for them to let me enter their environments.

The locals called me "docky." They told me that it was a very jovial form of calling me doctor, since they didn't like to call me by my name. At least, that was what I believed.

Visiting the mental hospital left me with a feeling of witnessing the days of slavery. It was pretty sad. There was an atmosphere of carelessness and inhumanity that was difficult to describe in words. Most of the patients were nude or nearly nude. The vast majority of them lay on the ground, covered by flies of all sizes. The rest of them were walking around the dirt patio.

There was a common room for women and another for men. They slept on the concrete floor, since the iron beds that were used at the beginning, over time, became weapons used by the patients. They all spent the day in the courtyard. They were taken to their respective rooms when the heat and the sun were very strong. There were barrels of water, from which they all drank with their hands.

As soon as I got inside the site, many of the patients surrounded me, trying to touch me and shake my hand. Regardless of their deplorable hygienic conditions, the gazes of those who did not "have it lost" begged for help. It was very difficult to control the helplessness of not being able to do something that could change their realities.

Learning what to suggest and what to do to improve neurological care, without detaching myself from the cruel reality, was a great professional challenge.

Walking, I tried to visit as many small communities, homes of all kinds and health centers as possible, trying to build in my mind a program that was capable of bringing benefits, without damaging feelings, culture and professional egos.

To visit remote places, I took the local buses. Each trip was an existential and cultural experience that carried a very unique idiosyncrasy.

In Lusaka, there were places for local foreigners, mainly from Europe and Japan, surrounded by great walls and military surveillance, with all kinds of amenities, including beautiful gardens, swimming pools, satellite dishes, nice cars, and nice houses. They were like a magical oasis in the middle of the desert. The contrast with the surroundings left much to be desired, and it was immoral and unfair.

There were also some foreigners mixed with the local population, who were extraordinary human beings, most of them belonging to missionary religious groups from different churches around the world. There were also other groups, of international origin, made up of health workers who worked in special centers for people with AIDS.

After four p.m. and on weekends, everyone closed the mind and the heart for anything that was different from what they were used to doing. Drinking beers during that time with them was what opened their minds, in a way.

Inside the room where I was sleeping, the nights were so dark that I experienced memories of other missionary adventures. Those memories were similar to what was happening to me, but with different intensities and connotations. In that darkness, I couldn't see my hand placed a few inches from my face. Sometimes I would wake up in the middle of the night, thinking that I was dead, since my mind was working, but I couldn't see my body.

Due to the insecurity around where my room was located, they made me lock myself inside my room with a large chain and a huge padlock. It was like putting myself in jail. From time to time, it gave me great scares when someone tried to open the door in the middle of the night. The bad thing was that every time that happened, I would stay awake for hours. After several weeks, I discovered that most of the people who went to play with my bedroom door were psychiatry patients who ran away at night. Since then, I just made sure to close the door tightly. Although they kept waking me at night, I went back to sleep without problems.

After a few weeks of knocking on doors and windows, I was able to get in touch with people who worked in the health area, not only from Zambia but also from Congo, Angola, Tanzania, Mozambique, Botswana, Malawi, and Namibia. The interest in learning and the willingness to seek the possibilities to do so, shown by the nurses, technicians and doctors in those other countries, was really inspiring for me.

The neurology instruction course that I had designed was very well received. We met daily at the facilities of the Chainama Medical Health Educational Community. We used three different classrooms. Classes began at seven a.m. and ended at four p.m. There was a twenty-minute break at nine thirty a.m. and a fifteen-minute break at two thirty p.m. There was a lunch break from twelve noon to one p.m.

In each classroom, there were people with more or less similar knowledge and medical background, and I was going from classroom to classroom, teaching different topics about the symptoms of the most common neurological entities in the west-central region of Africa, in addition to teaching how to perform the general neurological examination. While I left them alone, in one classroom they practiced with each other how to perform the neurological examination, and in the other one they were going over the ways explained to make neurological diagnoses. In the other classroom, I was talking about the most frequent diseases. Classes and practices were rotated in such a way that everyone could receive the same information, with degrees of difficulty according to their interests and abilities. Something that I tried to emphasize to each student was that they had to study themselves cognitively, emotionally, spiritually and professionally before trying to study neurology, since that was the key to being a good professional in that area of medicine.

There were a total of ninety-six students, with students from Zambia and the other seven countries that had been contacted. For four weeks I experienced elation – intellectually, emotionally, professionally and spiritually, but not physically. By six p.m., I was lying on my mattress, literally mindless. During the day, it was magical to witness the atmosphere permeated with a hunger to learn and improve.

It was fascinating to share with all those health professionals from different areas of Zambia and from neighboring countries. Their extraordinary desire to learn and to improve themselves was already marking the steps towards the success of the Zambia Project, which I was trying to implement.

By week six or seven, I was able to start writing the project report. By that time, I had already obtained important statistical data on health-related personnel – doctors, nurses, technicians, students, teachers, administrative personnel, and maintenance workers. The data was up to July 2002. The sad and surprising thing was to find in those data that 65% of all employees and 72% of all students were HIV positive. The doctor who was with me most of the time, his wife and his two children were also HIV positive. Five of the six doctors I had been in contact with since I arrived were HIV positive, and one of them had advanced AIDS.

By the end of the second month, the first society for neuropsychiatry had been integrated. The board of directors was composed of three psychiatrists, two pediatricians, two internists, two obstetricians, two clinicians, two rehabilitation technicians, and one administrator. The cooperation of a psychiatry professor from England, who had lived in Zambia since the 1950s was essential.

In Zambia, the mother and the eldest daughter had the same family rank and the same legal rights. Any member of the family who disobeyed or attacked the mother or eldest daughter was punished with thirty days in jail, for the first offense.

Malnutrition in the general population had been fought in recent years, thanks to a combined effort by the government and a local private company that sold a low-cost nutritional supplement "meheau" That food supplement came in four different fruit flavors. It was sold in plastic bottles. Each bottle contained 2,900 calories, balanced to meet daily carbohydrate, lipid and protein needs. Each 300cc bottle cost twenty-five US cents.

Japan was the country that was helping the Zambian government and people the most at that time. The government of Great Britain was donating the necessary material for schools, colleges, and universities.

In my walks in the surroundings, I had the great opportunity to once again enjoy the beautiful Jacaranda trees with their purple flowers. I saw them for the first time in Pretoria, South Africa, when I stayed there for a couple of days, for work reasons, in the late 1990s. They told me that during the English rule, more than 200,000 of those original trees from Zambia were planted in Pretoria.

Unfortunately, the drought of recent years had destroyed almost the entire maize crop, which was the main source of food for the inhabitants of this region of Africa. Their African cultural roots did not allow them to accept international aid with genetically modified grains.

The Zambia Project had achieved more goals than the proposed ones. What had been created and innovated was remaining to be put into action as time went by. It was time to let it be and let it grow with its people. The enthusiasm, the desire to improve and the professional concern to take what was learned to community action were already on the table and were constituting the engine of the project. I returned to Caracas by the same route on which I came.

Having been in a place where there was so much to do, it was impossible to leave without feeling that what was done was only of small significance, that it was lost in the intensity of the needs. But the gazes, enthusiasm, receptivity and commitment of the ninety-six students in the course left me with the feeling that seeds had been sown in fertile soil.

The smiles, the words and the moments shared with a large number of people, with a diversity of idiosyncrasies, were seeds sown in our Mother Earth – Gaia – for the benefit of all as a unit, as humanity, as brothers, as children of God.

This experience in Africa planted many seeds in me, which I was sure would grow over time. When one was in a place where there was so much to do, I think that trying to do it was what really mattered. Because if we didn't try, not only would we not know that we could do it, but we would continue to justify ourselves within the ideas, the desires, and the excuses.

You feel and want to do a lot, but when you start trying to do "the how much you feel and want," you realize that it is not the quantity of what is done, but the quality and the consciousness with which it is done, that makes the difference.

I left this continent smiling, knowing that I did not come to teach but to find excuses to be taught. I hoped that I had learned much more than I thought I had learned.

At the end of this third missionary experience, I had once again proven to myself that it was not about what I wanted to give, but about how much I wanted to receive from others.

Each and every one of us is missionaries, and perhaps our mission is simply to try to be the person we should be and not the person that we, or someone else, wants us to be.

Los Angeles – California

Time, in its relativity, had been determining the places where we have lived in recent years. Stability had recently begun to manifest itself in our family life. A sense of peace and security mixed with the air we breathed.

Now it was no longer me. Now the missionary mosquito had bitten my wife Carolina. And although on this occasion I was not the one who felt the itch to embark on a missionary adventure, I had no choice but to try to calm my wife's itch or start to scratch myself too.

Carolina had already begun to awaken, from time to time in recent years, to an illusion of life that was sleeping inside her. An illusion that she had shared with her mother since she was a child. She wanted to go on a mission to help needy children anywhere in the world.

Carolina graduated as a preschool teacher at the university in Venezuela. We used as "vanguard flag" "teacher/doctor-neurologist," emphasizing that we were two human beings committed to carrying out missionary work where it was needed.

Together we began to give shape to this illusion and began the search for alternatives. Like the rest of the people nowadays, we began our search through the Internet. We searched for any organization that offered opportunities for people who wanted to be lay missionaries, both in the United States and around the world. So we started filling out applications on the organizations' websites.

We were learning as we progressed in our search. We learned that we had to belong to a specific religion. Depending on our religion, the opportunities could materialize. We also learned that we had to be citizens of the country where the missionary organization was based. Our American citizenship would arrive in a couple of months, so we focused on US-based and Catholic organizations.

Organizations that were offering short-term opportunities included:

• Comboni – international organization named after its founder, Daniel Comboni, an Italian father who fought for the Vatican to accept lay missionaries on the African continent. It currently had priests and lay missionaries in Africa, Guatemala, Peru, Chile, among others.

• Cabrini –organization that had several centers within the United States and in different countries of the world, named after its founder, Francis Cabrini, a religious Italian who came to the United States. Her priority was immigrants, and they, as an organization, mainly offered help to immigrants in different countries of the world.

• The Franciscans and Salesians did not have open opportunities for laity at that time.

• The Society of African Missionaries –association that only worked with lay missionaries in Africa.

Unfortunately its headquarters in the United States was inactive.

•Maryknoll –organization mainly located in the United States, created by Maryknoll priests. They carried out missions in different countries of the world.

•Holly Cross –mainly located in the Dominican Republic and worked in conjunction with Fe y Alegría. Unfortunately, their headquarters in the United States had been closed for several years, but they accepted us as Venezuelans.

•Mission Doctors Association. Since 1959, Mission Doctors Association has trained, dispatched and supported Catholic physicians and their families who come from all over the United States to serve people of all faiths in some of the most underserved areas of the world.

We had telephone and Skype interviews with all of them, and personal interviews with the Franciscans and with Maryknoll. We also had the opportunity to visit the main office of the Comboni missionaries in Chicago. This last organization was really beautiful. The priests filled us with their wisdom and inner love, and the attention of those in charge of the program was really something special.

Later we went to an interview with the Mission Doctors Association in Los Angeles. That interview involved a thorough psychological evaluation as a prerequisite. They were three extremely intense days in Los Angeles. We had individual interviews in conjunction with meeting the clinical psychologist, who reviewed in detail with us, the psychological evaluations that we had carried out previously. They told us about Tanzania and the immense need that the country had for neurologists in a missionary center located in Ndanda, where a neurologist and a teacher were urgent and essential needs. After reviewing our resumes, checking our references, both personal and professional, having shared several days with us and having conducted multiple and varied interviews with different people, they offered us the opportunity to go as missionaries with their organization.

The commitment, initially, was for three years. We would have to be in Los Angeles before January 30, 2012, for a training period of about twenty weeks, and then by June we would be leaving for Tanzania. The Diocese of Mtwara in Tanzania would be responsible for us. They explained to us that the town of Ndanda was about three and a half hours from the nearest city where we could stock up on the basics, and the way to get there was on dirt roads and with potential mishaps, etc.

At the end of that training course, the archbishop of Los Angeles was going to accredit us as lay missionaries from the United States. With that credential, the Mission Doctors Association was going to apply for the respective visas of the countries to which we would go.

We returned to the west coast of Florida where we lived. The intricacies of disarming one reality, in order to launch us into another, began. We did not have much time left to think about the potential distance that could exist between our illusory idea of being lay missionaries in

Africa for a period of no less than three years and the real reality of what it was.

We had two cars. The newest one and recently bought only a few months ago, to be our Florida pearl, was given to our eldest son, Ricardo. By that time, we already had two children. The second was born in Waycross, Georgia, in 2003. His name was Rony Alberto, but we called him "Rony." He was extraordinary with his brother, and with us he was a son, a companion, and a friend. He taught us to be better human beings, while he showed us his daily idiosyncrasies.

Before beginning the changes involved in dismantling the house and reducing it to its minimum expression, we drove our Florida pearl, accompanied by our son Rony, to Manhattan, to leave both of them to Ricardo. Due to the pressure of the time, Carolina and I were flying back to Florida the next day.

Regarding the other car, which was already about eight years old, we did not know what was best for us – whether to donate it to an institution to help us with American taxes, or sell it, which was a bit complicated for us due to the short time we had to do so, in addition to the fact that what we would get from the sale of the car was not really going to solve anything.

The solution came to us when, one day, looking for storage to leave our important belongings – documents, books, family photographs, etc. – we stopped in a place near the house, and the manager showed us the physical spaces they had available. We had no idea of the cost of them. Prices were skyrocketing. Suddenly it occurred to us to ask the manager if we could use the car as part of payment. The manager's response was faster than our request. We ended up bartering the car for a three-and-a-half-year contract for an eight-by-eight-foot space.

There began one of the various odysseys which destiny had in store for us. We managed to fill the storage with almost literally no room for a pin. We managed to save some furniture and personal things that were already destined to be given away. Throughout that process, I was surprised by Carolina's capacity for detachment. We both enjoyed the happiness of the people who came to our house to take things away, without having to pay for them. In a couple of days we were reduced to two potential lay missionaries, each with a suitcase weighing no more than fifty pounds.

Days later we left for Los Angeles alone, accompanied by the aforementioned two suitcases. We were both inundated with a feeling that we were about to draw a line between what we knew we were and what we had no idea what we would be. But a magic illusion full of joy and happiness was pushing us forward, without letting us think or feel.

We arrived at The Mission House. That was a Catholic nunnery next to a church. The room they assigned to us, thank God, was that of a fat nun, since Carolina and I were able to fit in. The room – 3.3 by 2.4 meters – had a bed large enough for both of us to sleep like nuns; that is, looking at the ceiling and without moving much, so as not to fall. There was a sink with a little mirror, a rather small desk on the other side, and a chair where half a person could sit. Between the two rooms there was a shower on one side and a WC on the other side to be shared.

Within hours of arriving, I learned that dwarf nuns lived in that convent. When I went to take a shower, I had to go sideways into the space where the shower was, and the shower jet reached between my navel and my chest. There was no room to bend down even a bit, which left me no choice but to use both hands together to push the water towards my face.

A new adventure was beginning to appear. We began to live with nineteen other lay missionaries.

In the midst of the structured and demanding training program, the humor managed to intermingle. On Carolina's birthday, we were all in a twenty-four-hour meditation of total silence. You couldn't talk, you couldn't receive calls, you couldn't read the emails they sent you, or browse Facebook. The day you meet Carolina, you will understand the touch of humor in all that. At the end of the twenty-four hours of silence, the first thing Carolina told me was that she had never felt "so nun," and she already thought she was one of the nuns of the Discalced Carmelite congregation."

Thursday, March 1, was our exam and interview to obtain American citizenship, a fundamental requirement to be able to go on missionaries. We had to travel to Orlando and rent a car to get to the immigration offices in

Tampa. Our appointment was scheduled for nine fifteen a.m.

Carolina went first, with a female officer. She said that as soon as she sat in the chair in front of the officer's desk, the officer began to ask the pertinent questions. When the officer asked her where she lived, Carolina very cleverly answered that at that time she lived in Los Angeles, because she was in a training program to go as a missionary to Africa. She showed her a letter from the director of the Mission Doctors Association program, explaining motives and asking for the courtesy of seeing if we could be sworn in that day, as we were leaving as missionaries.

Carolina said that after reading the letter, the officer got up and went to speak with the general manager. Carolina waited for about ten to fifteen minutes until the officer entered her office again and told her: "We very rarely do this, but this time we are going to make an exception and we are going to swear both of you in."

While I was still in the middle of my interview, the general director came in, accompanied by the officer who had interviewed Carolina, and they asked me to follow them. I looked at the officer who was interviewing me, and amid a not-so-pleased facial expression, he jerked his head for me to go behind them.

I followed them, and they directed me to go into an office. It was the director's office. Carolina was sitting in one of the armchairs in the living room, and she told me what was happening. In a few minutes, the director entered. We stood in front of him. He spoke to us very nicely for about five minutes, and later he swore us in as US citizens, reading the provisions of the immigration law.

At 10. 05 a.m., we left through the door of the immigration building, ready to proceed as missionaries. As good missionaries and new American citizens, we celebrated by eating hamburgers at McDonald's.

In the months that followed, on several occasions we were caught between the storms of our own mixed thoughts and feelings, where family, work, friends, and loved ones were gusts of wind and heavy rain.

The process of reinventing ourselves continued day by day. We were leaving behind what we were, to find what we thought we should be, in order to try to reach what we were supposed to want.

On May 21, we had the graduation ceremony as lay missionaries. It was a beautiful church ceremony. Missionary rings were imposed, and credentials were handed out.

The visas and the corresponding procedures for our arrival in Tanzania were delayed more than expected. We were waited in Los Angeles for a few days, but due to the absence of positive news, we decided to go to New York to be with our two children until the necessary papers arrived.

Seeing them again and being all together made our trip to Tanzania a little more difficult. Rony's adaptation to the conditions in which Ricardo lived was not easy. But Ricardo gave him the feeling of belonging, which was so important to him during our absence. Seeing each other, bathing him, hugging him and playing with him again filled him with an energy that was conspicuously absent by being separated from us.

On June 10, we said goodbye to our children, the human son Ricardo and the Golden Retriever son Rony, to begin the journey to Dar es Salaam, Tanzania.

The intensive preparation course to become a missionary in the United States was extraordinarily good and multifaceted in its essence. University professors, members of the UN, people belonging to missionary groups, priests from different congregations, nuns, etc., participated by sharing their knowledge and experiences with the whole group.

If I could summarize in a few words the crux of what it meant to climb the steps necessary to embark on missionary activity, I would say that it was all a matter of conscience, attention, commitment, spirit of adventure and hopes of meeting you on the road, with the catapults that would launch you into the world of the realities that you dream and desire for yourself and for all the people you love and who accompany you through the journey of life.

Religions and creeds are like the trees in a forest. Everyone has the possibility, according to his/her free will, to get close to the tree that he/she likes the most to be sheltered by it. It is important that one protect, care for and enjoy the chosen tree, as well as the benefits of sheltering under its shade.

Perhaps there are trees that are interpreted as stronger, bigger, more beautiful and with a greater capacity to shelter people under their shade, but the reality is that each tree is unique in the mind and heart of the one that accepted it to shelter him/her, for the one who venerates it – for the one who has the faith and the hope that under its shadow there will be no troubles in life.

But below the surface, of that surface that we cannot see, the roots of all the trees are subtly mixed, as they all feed on the same substrate –the substrate of God's love.

Each tree in the forest represents a truth. There is no truth the same as another, but similar. What must be taken into account is that all truths feed on the same substrate.

Clinging to a single tree or a single truth is losing the notion that you live in a forest. To think that your truth is the only truth, is to live in black and white, with the illusion that the more shades of gray you can appreciate in your life, the more spirituality you profess and the closer you are to the divinity that created you.

Enjoying the forest as such allows you to have not only white, black and all shades of gray, but to experience the world of unlimited beauties of the colors.

Through trusting in what we know, we can enter the world of what we do not know, knowing that we know where we are going.

Africa - Ndanda, Tanzania

At the airport, waiting to leave for Dar es Salaam, amid the tears of a very difficult emotional farewell, smiles began to intermingle. We could not say exactly that they were smiles of joy, but rather that they were smiles of anguish of falling into a reality that moved between threads totally unknown to us.

The only thing we knew was that Brother Damian, who belonged to the Congregation of the Benedictine Fathers, was going to Dar es Salaam to meet us at the airport. In the telegram we had from the congregation, it also said: 'Look for a man who will have a sign that says Enrique and Carolina. In Dar es Salaam, they will receive further instructions.'

At that moment, we began to fall into the reality that we were not going on a crazy missionary adventure, but that we were crazy people, who with the excuse of being lay missionaries, were in search of adventures, without having a clear idea of what adventure meant or what it could potentially mean.

I didn't know what concept Tanzania would have of the United States. But in immigration, with the income form you had to pay fifty dollars, for holders of passports from any country in the world, except for holders of passports from the United States, who had to pay one hundred dollars.

As we left the airport, we saw the sign that said, 'Enrique and Carolina.' Carolina and I looked directly into each other's eyes as a reflex action and said simultaneously: "You have to have faith."

We were picked up by a very nice priest, about eighty-five years old, of German origin. We spent the night in a room of the Benedictine residence in Dar es Salaam. The next day we left by plane for the city of Mtwara. Unfortunately the plane was overweight, and right there at the foot of the plane, we had to take some things out of the suitcases, which we then put in the backpack we were carrying. The priest who dropped us off at the airport took our bags, telling us that in one to three days they would be with us in Ndanda.

In Mtwara, they would pick us up to move us, by land, to Ndanda. For unknown reasons, it took them three days to search for us. We took this advantage to buy two simple cell phones and getting to know the surroundings.

In our minds and hearts, the intention had already been engendered to carry out a missionary program in Ndanda. In its beginnings, it would be based, mainly, on the example that we would give through our living and our daily work.

It was very clear in our minds that the need to be quite aware of its history, its social structure, its customs, its values, its religious perceptions, its intellectual discernment and its moral parameters was essential to achieve a positive response in the community in which we were going to live.

We would try, of course, to promote the concept of integral health, where the spiritual, the physical, the medical, the psychological, the social and the cultural were able to manage to intertwine with each other, without damaging each other in the attempt.

We would arrive at Ndanda and be at the disposition and under the orders of the Benedictine Congregation in charge of the Ndanda hospital, in the Mtwara region. The care of the sick was the primary priority in the statutes of the Benedictine Congregation, written in the sixth century. Since then, Benedictine missionaries had dedicated themselves to caring for the sick, visiting them at their home, opening health clinics to care for them, etc. Over time, those health dispensaries grew in the quality of their services, becoming hospitals.

The commitment of this congregation was to serve all patients with affection and love, overcoming any problem or difficulty that would interfere, in relation to human resources and the available materials.

According to the information we had been given, at the Ndanda hospital, two Benedictine nuns were working as surgeons, both graduated from German universities. Since September 1, 1998, the Sister Thecla Stinnesbeck Memorial Hospital Foundation was in charge of the hospital. The hospital had four hundred beds distributed in four patient wards.

In a region such as southern Tanzania, predominantly Islamic, but with a social and pastoral openness, missionary services were highly desired and appreciated.

As a doctor, at that time, I thought that I was very clear that dignity and responsibility in the practice of medicine would never be sufficiently understood or adequately expressed unless medicine was practiced with implicit love at all times – for the truth and being ambassadors of life.

I also thought that, as doctors, we had to be and express who we really were, bluntly, unpretentious and fearless. As doctors we also needed to learn, on a daily basis, to separate ourselves from dualities: right and wrong, good and bad, and so on. It was in this constant learning that we could teach, and perhaps in that teaching we would be able to understand.

On the same day we arrived in Ndanda, I had a meeting with the hospital administrator. There came, straight into my face, the first blow of the disorganization – the half-truths and the half-lies from the director of the Mission Doctors Association. The administrator, very annoyed, told me that he had remarked, very well and on several occasions to the director of the program, when she visited them about 6 months ago, to specify the details of our internship in the community, and that the doctors she was thinking to bring had, as primary requirement, the ability to speak and understand Swahili well, the language in which all communication was carried out in the hospital.

They did not have any kind of staff available to serve as a translator.

While waiting for an intensive course in Swahili, offered by the Mission Doctors Association, the first weeks I spent reviewing inpatients of surgery and in the areas of operating rooms, as well as in the obstetrics area, where there were staff who spoke a little English and who occasionally communicated with me. All communication was in Swahili. My language was my looks, my smiles, and some hand gestures. My main role was reduced to observing and trying to pay attention to as many details as possible in patients.

Culture and poverty set the guidelines for medical care, where the patient remained in precarious conditions. Lack of manners and poor hygienic conditions were an aggravating factor. In the midwifery area, there were typically five to six women totally naked on plastic mats in labor, and some aborting alone. There was no parenteral hydration. They were orally hydrated, and there were no pain medications of any kind.

The impotence of not being able to help as I wanted made me feel like an accomplice in everything I was observing around me. The Benedictine mottos with which the care of the sick had been established in the first place had already disappeared. Since the government took control of the hospital from them, only about four to five months before we arrived, the deterioration was in free fall. There were no longer any medical personnel from the Benedictine congregation working at the hospital. The surgeon nuns, obstetricians, as well as those who were in charge of the hospital, had already left by the time we arrived.

Surgical technicians and general medicine natives of the area exercised the functions of the doctor nuns who were no longer there. The administration was now in the hands of civilian personnel from the province. Only a few Tanzanian-born Benedictine nuns remained, in certain nursing care areas.

With regard to Carolina, she spent her time walking around and offering her help to whoever needed it. After several weeks, she began teaching English to interested parties, on an individual basis.

We felt already, in the first weeks of being in Ndanda, that the realities were strongly corroding our thoughts and feelings. Our instincts were telling us that for the better, but our thinking and feeling still did not know how to define it. When we left the United States to come to Africa, with the idea of working as lay missionaries, we thought that we were going to work long hours a day on a great mission. Unfortunately, we were totally wrong.

Perhaps we did not understand it at the time, that the issue was not about how much we would do, since "doing" is relative, and maybe everything was about "being." Doing, for us here in Ndanda, was so full of cultural and linguistic limitations that it was turning into an insignificance. The being, with the very limited doing, was in a constant battle, where our expectations, our intentions and our realities were also struggling.

It is the "being" that lay missionary is all about. The being ourselves without denying our beliefs, our acquired knowledge and our cultural roots; it is to be, twenty-four hours a day, trustworthy examples of the interrelation of our divinity and the divinity found in people and in the nature around us; it is learning to love ourselves through loving others; it is about trust, hope, compassion, forgiveness, tolerance, understanding, and boasting in the truth that is in us and in others.

It seems that being a lay missionary is about an experience that makes it easier for us to live experiences. Perhaps it is just our intention of wanting to believe that we are needy. I believe that being a missionary is learning to understand that there are not really missionaries, but rather people seeking missions among the life missions of others who are in different conditions, which we have classified from our angle of observation as precarious.

One of the most fascinating things about experiencing diversity was seeing excellence emerge from within it. A Benedictine priest from Colombia, who spoke perfect German and Swahili, became our friend, our co-missionary, our guide, and our companion –the much-loved "Father Jorge," as he allowed us to call him. With him we went to the homes of people with neurological problems to help them.

Using the imagination to implement devices for rehabilitation, ambulation, support and to improve their general conditions, stimulated our minds and hearts, making us feel that we were love in action. Visiting the homes of people in need of our attention, with Father Jorge, made us feel, for the first time since our arrival in Ndanda, that we were missionaries.

As a synchronism of the energies involved in our earthly existences, since we began the visits with Father Jorge, which we were doing mainly after three o'clock in the afternoon, other alternatives appeared for Carolina. The very night of our first visit, the director of the Benedictine nuns asked Carolina to design an intensive English course for the novices. And the next morning, she started giving them English classes, every morning, four hours a day.

Carolina was happy to feel useful and needed.

We had the great opportunity to establish a special friendship with the Abbot of the congregation, named Dyonis. He was of German origin and had lived in Ndanda Abbey for many years. It was fascinating to be with him and to walk beside him. He constantly conveyed a unique sweetness and peace. Being next to him made us experience intense love and energy, full of divine beauty.

In that Benedictine community, we were called "Daktari Wulff and Mama Carolina."

The Tanzanian people who lived in the province where we were staying were easygoing in their way of being. Their culture was orchestrated primarily by verbal communication. When you met them, they greeted you, and they talked to you about everything, and the last thing they asked you after one or two hours of being with you was your name. They believed in stories a lot and enjoyed them a lot; they didn't like to read. They liked telling stories so much that sometimes when they arrived late or didn't do something they should have done, they told you a story. The vast majority of the time it wasn't true, but you never confronted them, you just enjoyed them. When a family member was ill, probably few went to visit him/her in the hospital, but if he/she died, the whole family was mobilized for the burial. They loved celebrations of all kinds. It was important for them to own a piece of land, and even if they did not cultivate it or no longer lived in that area, they continued to maintain it, because the day they died, they would be buried in that land.

The Tanzanians were very calm people. They sought peace, they loved that tourists visited, and they gave everyone a unique welcome. They think a lot about today and little about tomorrow; they harvested for the moment and not for the future. They believed a lot in witchcraft and magical things that happened in life. For them, everything that happened to us in life is because we did something that caused it. They worshiped the ancestors and used them as intermediaries of God – as Catholics used the saints. Many times they even made sacrifices by offering them to the ancestors who were buried in the front of the house, so that they were always sending their wisdom to their relatives.

The concept of time for them was different from ours. For example, a week ago the education commissioner for the area said that he was going to go to school at ten o'clock in the morning, for a meeting with the teachers and the Benedictine congregation, among whom we were. He arrived at twelve noon and at no time made any excuses. The higher the hierarchy, not only did you make fewer excuses, but you took longer.

The vast majority were Muslims, although Christianity was growing in recent decades. Matriarchy ruled those areas of southern Tanzania. There were a large number of women alone with their children. In their culture, rituals were very important.

When they spat on your hand, it was the most beautiful thing that someone could do, because it meant that they were offering you the most beautiful thing about him/her. They believed that their saliva contained the essence of the most intimate part of their divinity and their person. This was one of the parts of their culture where sometimes you wished that they didn't like you so much.

It was already about three months since we arrived in Ndanda. Other opportunities had opened up for Carolina. She started going with two Benedictine sisters, every Monday, to visit the twelve preschools that belonged to the Benedictine parish. Carolina told me that the children went from eight a.m. until 12 noon. The teaching method was the Montessori method, the same method that Carolina used when she worked as a teacher in Venezuela.

Benedictine sisters had the opportunity to learn this method of education for children in Amsterdam in the 1940s, with the extraordinary Italian scientific educator, Maria Montessori, who was the one who designed and established it for the benefit of all the children of the world.

Years later, this method of education was implanted in the children of Ndanda

The sisters brought them bags of special flour prepared with ground corn, cassava, powdered milk, and salt. What they brought them was enough to feed them for the whole week. The flour was mixed with hot water and was left to cook for about ten minutes, then it was given to the children at ten a.m.

Listening to Carolina telling us the minutia about how they got to the preschools made us laugh a lot. The nun who was driving was originally from Mtwara province, and she was super joyful person. She loved to go at full speed in her 1950 English Land Rover. That vehicle, that had survived being driven by emotive nuns for many decades through inhospitable terrains, had two very deteriorated front seats where the nuns sat, and in the back were two aluminum benches without cushions, where Carolina sat among the provisions.

Carolina said that they were three women in a 4 x 4, driving over rough terrain, and they were jumping along the dirt roads, with holes, trees and branches crossing it. As expected, it was my turn to act as a doctor the rest of the week with Carolina, trying to help her with the neck and back pain that she had after arriving that day. On Monday night she was not complaining of any pain, due to the adrenaline that was generated in her body, counting the emotions of the children and of hers, when seeing them and being with them.

The children ran out to greet them, and when they returned to their classrooms, they sang welcome songs. Being in contact and sharing with so many children literally illuminated her soul. She said that her looks, her smiles and her shrieks of laughter made her feel in the presence of God.

The moment arrived, and in a few days we would leave for Arusha, in the north of Tanzania, to begin the intensive course in Swahili, organized by the director of the program, from Los Angeles. The same day that we arrived at the Swahili school, we were given a written and oral evaluation. Despite the four to five hours a day that we studied on our own, from books and notes that were loaned to us in Ndanda, we were told that we would both be in the beginner's class.

Due to the pressure, I had to learn, as soon as possible, to communicate in Swahili. I went to speak with the director of the school and explained my situation to her. Despite the fact that she explained to me that learning Swahili was not easy and deserved a coupling to the new sounds while learning the corresponding grammar, my distressing situation filled me with arrogance, thinking that with my experience of studying, I could advance faster, and so they put me in the intermedium level.

Both Carolina and I became paranoid people studying Swahili. In addition to the eight hours a day of classes, we studied and did the corresponding tasks until midnight, and then we got up at four in the morning to study the classes that would be given to us that day. On weekends, we studied under a strict schedule of fourteen hours a day, and we left only a few hours on Saturday and Sunday to rest and walk around.

Those weeks of studying under pressure, with some study schedules that were swinging themselves between stupidity and dementia, were not easy and consumed us emotionally and mentally.

Carolina wondered why the organization had sent us to a place where we do not speak their language, as we had decided to give those three years of our lives to help the needy who lived in precarious conditions. She knew that I also questioned that. I avoided, as much as possible, not putting it into words so as not to add fuel to the fire.

The balance, as expected, was broken. What I never imagined was the way it was broken. With about four days left until we finished the course, in the middle of one of the classes I had a neurological experience that really scared me. It was about ten a.m. when I suddenly lost my ability to express myself in Swahili. I couldn't even articulate a word. I sneakily left the class and began to walk through the gardens to wait for it to pass. I tried to stay silent. I spent the next two hours trying to observe my surroundings, not trying to speak, and avoiding thinking about what was happening to me. What I could not avoid was the constant checking of my motor and sensory abilities, which apparently were doing fine.

At noon it was time to go to lunch, and Carolina saw me walking but not in the direction of the dining room. She approached me, accompanied by one of her English-speaking classmates. They started talking to me in English, and not only did I not understand them, but I also couldn't express myself in English. Immediately I answered them in Spanish, trying to make it as a joke, and I made faces so that they understood that I was going to the room.

Carolina, as expected, immediately realized that something was wrong, and she said goodbye to her friend and followed me into the room. I tried to explain what was happening to me, in Spanish, but I didn't want to go into much detail. My thinking was almost entirely as a neurologist, and I was focused on diagnosing what could be happening to me. I told her that I was very tired and that I was not going to have lunch or go to classes in the afternoon, since I was going to take a nap. She accepted what I told her and left me in the room.

When she left, I bathed and went to bed. I fell asleep for several hours. When I woke up, Carolina was by my side, seeing me, of course, very anguished at not knowing what was happening to me. I still couldn't express myself in English. We decided to get out and head to Arusha city center for a walk and dinner.

I kept trying to try to diagnose myself, in the middle of a disguised silence. I was balancing not only the symptoms presented with the potential diagnoses, but also the potentialities and possibilities of using medical services in Arusha.

At dinner, understanding and expressing myself in English returned almost immediately. A slight difficulty in articulating the beginning of some words in Spanish began to manifest itself. Trying to stay objective, practical and realistic, without losing control of my emotions, was not easy. I did not want my thoughts to be influenced by fear, impelling me to an action that was not intelligently studied according to the circumstances.

I did not go to the last few classes of the course. I walked through the gardens, speaking Spanish aloud until it normalized over the next few days. I didn't try to read or say another word in Swahili.

I laughed at myself, thinking that if I told others about it, they would think that they had turned me into a Swahili witch, and I would end up being seen by a witch doctor.

When I returned to Ndanda, I no longer had a problem with what little I had learned in Swahili.

I will try to put in a few words, without giving it too much thought at a neurological level, what could have happened to me. As I mentioned earlier in this book, I was born with a neurolinguistic condition known as developmental dyslexia. This condition, associated with my known difficulty in learning a second language, demonstrated by "experts" when I just recently graduated as a doctor, to do a postgraduate degree in Cambridge, England… were "voluntarily" put by me in "a torture dungeon," mainly influenced by my poverty of conscience in relation to everything related to learning Swahili. If I were not a neurologist, I would think that there was a short circuit in my brain due to excess electrical charges coming from many parts.

Upon arrival at the house in Ndanda, we found that all our clothes that we had left in a locked closet had been stolen. Unfortunately, I had left my missionary ring, my watch, a jackknife, glasses, and other personal things. We went to tell the administrator, who was the one who told us to keep things there and gave us the key to the closet. With a passive attitude, he told us that that happens sometimes and is part of the culture. We were literally experiencing, once again, being light of luggage. In the following weeks, we saw people, students and hospital workers with our clothes on. One had the missionary ring, someone had my watch, and some students wore Carolina's clothes. It was a unique and different experience. We told ourselves, with a strange humor full of acceptance, that at least we were already more part of the community, since part of us was already mixed among them.

It was a whole process of cultural adaptation, that single fact of seeing what *was* yours, in others, without your consent, and then giving your consent, under the pressure of the influences of the environment where we were, and accepting that our things were no longer our things, but they were their things. And if we identified them as our things, it would generate a negative reaction against us, by the mere fact of insinuating that their things could be our things.

One of those mornings, we went to see a group of children who belonged to the parish program called

Uzima. They were HIV-positive children, many orphans, either without a father or mother, some without both. The program was offering them, in addition to their medicines and transportation to the hospital when they needed it, information regarding their illness, recreational and educational activities, etc. The Uzima program was also helping HIV-positive or AIDS-infected women and men.

The little children called me "Mzungu," which means white man, and they called Carolina by her name. It was easy for them to pronounce her name, which shares similarities with Swahili. It was a very nice sensation and at the same time so full of family mysticism, hearing, everywhere we passed, the little children shouting, "Carolina, Carolina."

That night, the manager came to our house to talk to us and brought with him six beers. In the middle of the conversation and after he already had three of the beers, he suddenly told us that he had to tell us the truth. Carolina and I were speechless, waiting to see what the truth was. He told us that the director of our program, on her visit months before our arrival, told him that the main reason for us to come to Ndanda was that Carolina was going to be in charge of the education of the four children of the couple of doctors who supposedly were coming with us. And that I was going to be the support of the two doctors. The man was an internist-pulmonologist, and she was a pediatrician. That was why they did not know what to do with us, since that family delayed their arrival to Ndanda for six months. The only thing that we thought to reply was to thank him for all the help he had given us.

It was second direct hit to the face, of the half-truths, the half-lies and the lack of honesty towards us from the director of the Mission Doctors Association.

As things of destiny, Carolina had been speaking a few days ago with one of the friends who had taken the training course with us in Los Angeles, who was in Kenya. Her missionary companion had returned to California, and she thought that we could do a great job where she was. She spoke of working in a hospital that was about twenty minutes from where she was, in a town called Nkubu, five hours from Nairobi, and where there was a great need for doctors and people to help in the hospital.

The priest in charge of the Nkubu parish had tried to convince the organization, since he learned that we arrived in Tanzania, to send us to where he was, since the Nkubu hospital was in great need of a doctor like me.

The priest somehow managed to get my resume, so he already had some extra information. The missionary friend, in her illusion of having us there, began to secretly sell the idea. They used, as a great aggravation in their favor, that everyone in the hospital spoke English. Without us mentioning anything that the administrator told us, we let things flow on their own. The situation generated many mixed feelings. We were identified with the people of Ndanda, with Father Jorge, with the abbot of the congregation Dyonis, and with the priests and sisters of the Benedictine congregation in Ndanda. We had connected with many people who had been super special to us. We wanted to stay in or around Ndanda. We had considered running a peripheral clinic, which mainly cared for people with leprosy and where local women would have their children. The director of the Benedictine sisters was working the logistics.

Meanwhile, the priest of Nkubu and our missionary friend managed, without our participation, to convince the organization. In less than a week, we were leaving for Nairobi. When the news was known at the Ndanda hospital, there was no reaction whatsoever.

A response of mixed emotions, expressed feelings, tears and good wishes on the part of the Benedictine sisters and priests, as well as the people we had met in the community, not only countered the reaction of the hospital but filled us with joy in the midst of great nostalgia.

A pain that seemed to be generated in our cells flooded us when leaving Ndanda. Between tears, five months of all kinds of emotions and experiences lived had passed at high speed. In an attempt to calm so many emotions and feelings, we tried to convince ourselves that it was not a goodbye, but that it was only a see you later.

There were no victims or victimizers, and there was no dramatization. There was only love shared with those who joined us in the action.

Ndanda had received a large part of us. We just hoped that they would act like seeds. Her wisdom, her realities, her experiences, her mysticism, her tradition in time, her

Benedictine mission and her people remained as seeds in our hearts and in our minds.

Like smoke that rises to the sky to dissipate in the air without leaving traces, cultural oddities, inconsistencies, half-truths, half-lies, inaccuracies, frustrated utilizations, honesty imperfections, confusion and uncertainties were left.

Africa - Nkubu, Kenia

Our arrival in Nairobi was very warm and full of joy. Our friend and the priest who had processed our entire transfer were exemplary with us. Perhaps, without them knowing it, they gave us a feeling of belonging, which were awakening illusions, plans and favorable forecasts.

To take the path that would lead us to Nkubu, a large part of the city of Nairobi had to be crossed, which allowed us not only to feel like tourists, but to get to know each other through multivariate conversations. Nairobi traffic that day was really heavy. It took us a little over three hours to cross the city.

The priest really became an incessant source of energy generation. In addition to his cordiality towards us, he truly tried his best to make our arrival a great event, so that we would feel everything as a warm welcome. He wanted us to feel loved and important. He did not want us to suffer, a word that he repeated over and over again.

Carolina's eyes were flooded with joy and peace. She looked calm, as if a great weight had been lifted from her shoulders. She told me, smiling, how great it was to have the feeling of being in a place where we were welcome.

The priest was very excited that we were going to take the first recently inaugurated highway that was being built in Kenya. They called it the "super highway." In his healthy and enthusiastic joy, we passed, twice, through the first tunnel built in Kenya, which had been inaugurated just a few days before our arrival.

We continued our journey until we reached the arish of the priest – the Parish of St. Massimo, in Meru. The priest did not miss an opportunity to stop on the way to greet people and to buy things.

The plane landed at 9.10 a.m. at Nairobi airport, and we would arrive at Meru at 9.20 p.m. We passed the hospital and the town where we would live. We would stay in the Parish of St. Massimo, while the priest arranged the logistics.

The next morning, we went with the priest to visit the primary school, which was on the parish grounds. There were thirty-six to thirty-eight students per classroom, with their respective teacher. There were seven classrooms. The joy and dynamism of the students of all ages and genders was moving. In the parish and in the surrounding towns, the only ones "discolored" were the missionary friend, Carolina and me. In other words, it was difficult for us to go unnoticed. Within a few days, the whole area knew what we were doing, how we laughed, how we walked and where we were.

When we walked through the school, all the students ran out to surround us and touch us. It was a fascination for them, besides greeting us, touching us, shaking hands after they spit on their palms, and in my case, pulling the hairs on my arms.

At midmorning, we went to mass in the parish church, which was quite large. It was great. We entered dancing and singing African songs, which we did not understand, with dozens and dozens of women. We all reached the altar in procession, and then we went to the benches which were already assigned for us. The little boys and girls were escaping from their benches to sit between us, to such an extent that on the bench where we sat, which was for four to six people at the most, there were about twelve to fourteen little boys and girls with us, sitting on our seats, legs, and between us, one on top of the other.

The next morning, we left early for the Nkubu hospital, where I would have a meeting with the doctors at nine a.m. The hospital was a half-hour drive from where we were. It was a strange feeling, riding in the car with the priest, since the car was very luxurious. A late model seven-seat Lexus SUV, and the priest stopped everywhere so they could see us. That day, in a town about fifteen minutes from Nkubu, he parked practically in the middle of the main street and got out, supposedly to look for things, which would not take more than a couple of minutes.

The three of us stayed inside the truck with the windows down. We felt like a new TV in a store window, with everyone stopping to see us. Time passed, and I was worried that I would be late for the meeting at the hospital. After our missionary patience began to run out – that is, after more than an hour and a half of waiting – I walked out to look for him, trying to guess where he might be.

I got into some buildings, went down some stairs and found a store, half hidden, where they sold very nice, brand-name men's clothing. I went in with the idea of asking if by any chance they knew where the priest might be. To my surprise, and much more to the surprise of the two owners of the store and especially for the priest, I found them drinking whiskey while they sold imported suits and shirts to the priest. It was the only time I saw the priest with the color of my skin.

For days, the priest questioned, interrogated and even harassed the missionary friend to find out how I found him in that little store. For some reason, the father was left with the idea that I had the ability to get into his head.

We were staying in a little house in the hospital area. It was a Catholic hospital founded by the sisters of the Consolata congregation. It depended on the Archbishopric of Meru and was administered by two priests and a nun.

The experiences lived during the first week were truly wonderful, spiritual and full of wisdom of simple and noble people. The welcome to Kenya had really been something we never expected. They did not leave us alone for a minute. They were super grateful that we were there, and they were willing to work with us and asked us to do all kinds of projects for the good of the community.

They showed a condescension and a special interest in listening to us and allowing us to help them. They constantly showed their appreciation that we had left our family and comforts to be there with them. All of that made Carolina recover all her fortitude, her energies and her missionary strength to the dimensions that she had always wanted. She felt that she was opening the doors of Africa for her desire to help others.

Kenya welcomed us with a lot of love and with great potential for activities for us to carry out. Carolina told me that she was at the foot of a new challenge, in a country with different customs, with another mentality, with another ideology. She was very happy with the new opportunity to explore our inner divinity in the search to experience the divinity of others in their daily lives.

In general terms, the hospital consisted of five buildings with concrete block walls, about forty meters long by ten meters wide, with roofs of zinc or asbestos. One was for the surgery area, with an operating room and thirty beds for patients, and another for the maternity area, with a delivery room and thirty beds for patients, There was another for adult hospitalization with forty-five beds, and another for the hospitalization of children, which consisted of forty-five beds. The outpatient area contained five cubicles to examine patients, as well as the pharmacy and waiting areas. It was a new concept for great potential, which was already being generated in my mind and in my heart.

The day after we arrived in Nkubu, I was already sitting at seven a.m. in the outpatient room, discussing the cases of the evening and the night before, which were being presented to me. It was fascinating for me, since there were doctors and many students, and above all it allowed me to teach.

From nine a.m. to two p.m., I was making rounds to the patients in the area of surgery, maternity, hospitalization of adults and children, with the respective doctors and students in charge of the patients. I felt fulfilled and transported in dimensions of patient management that have always fascinated me, where I sought to offer the best according to the possibilities. There were all types of pathology, from malaria, leprosy, complications of AIDS, dengue, which were the most frequent infectious diseases, to isolated cases of rabies, cerebrovascular accidents, epilepsy of all types, as well as characteristic cases of chronic systemic and metabolic disorders.

Teaching was based mainly on the integration of diagnostic possibilities and on trying to objectify, as much as possible, those possibilities, with limited resources and the design of therapeutic alternatives that included everything accessible, including homeopathy, allopathic medicines, prayers, witchcraft, and any alternative that could improve the patient's conditions. From time to time, fascinating cases with neurological pathologies, unique to the tropics, would appear.

After having lunch with Carolina at home, I gave classes to the students at the nursing school, which existed as part of the hospital, from three p.m. to five p.m. After five p.m., Carolina and I walked out of the hospital area to explore the surroundings and mingle with the people.

It was very difficult for us not to arouse people's curiosity. One morning, Carolina returned home unexpectedly and found the hospital guardian checking our belongings in the room where we were sleeping. The hospital director said that it was part of the culture, when we let him known about this situation. The culture of Ndanda was now manifesting itself in Nkubu.

As a luxury artifact, we had a plastic water filter that the missionary companion had brought from the United States. The water we were drinking was brown. After we were filtered it several times, it was beige in color.

The hospital was supported by donations from non-governmental organizations and private sectors. International organizations, like the one we belonged to, were of great help, since they brought specialized doctors. They didn't give them a salary, only housing and the bare minimum so that they could feed themselves. There were doctors who came for periods of one or two months. The doctors who worked in the hospital were clinical officers. They studied for two to four years in technical schools, and then they started working in the hospitals.

When we walked around and in the same area of the hospital, we were invaded, from time to time, by the strange feeling, and at the same time interesting in its essence, of being different, since we were the only white people in the entire town and in the surrounding areas. The vast majority of people, when seeing us, shouted, "Mzungus" – which meant white person – and we greeted them with smiles and body language. It was a strange feeling of friendly racism.

The priest in charge of the hospital and the parish priest of St. Massimo met with me to fill out the application to practice medicine in Kenya. They explained to me that it was better for the hospital if I had the official Kenyan medical license, and not just the one of missionary doctor. Apparently they already had my resume and copies of my credentials and diplomas. Being certified by the American Board of the specialty and with the credentials that I had, I would be able to receive an official permit for five years, and then they would give me the Kenyan medical license. I was enthusiastic about the constancy in time, at least, for the next few years.

Carolina was very happy that she had begun working at the area's Comprehensive Care Center, a program that comprehensively addressed the needs of HIV and AIDS patients and their families. The center was treating an average of one hundred patients daily – children and adults. The care was really comprehensive. At eight a.m., the patients were already seated on wooden benches on a cement-floored patio, waiting for the first hour-long session. There were components of education, spiritual growth, and moral, familial, and existential support.

The session was given in Swahili, by social workers and nurses.

Later they were assessed individually, for the comprehensive medical evaluation. Nurses took their vital signs, reviewed treatments, and provided the respective medications and food supplements. Those patients that the nurses thought needed it, were assessed by clinical officers. Like all low-income public hospitals, many patients, either alone or with a family member or with their young children, could remain sitting on the wooden benches for four to six hours. The expressions of resignation and sadness were alarming. For Carolina, this was the hardest part. She could understand and speak Swahili quite a bit, so she was able to help more effectively.

On one of our hikes, late one afternoon, we left a little earlier than usual and decided to try new paths. While we were passing near a school, where there were at least 80 to 100 little boys and girls, from first to fourth grade, they began to shout: "Mzungu, Mzungu, Mzungu," while they were running like a flock towards us to greet us. There were some so small that in the middle of the race they fell, and the others passed over them. Upon reaching our side, they began to pull Carolina's hair and the hair of my arms, to take a souvenir, while others struggled to shake the hand that they had previously spat on.

Those who could not touch us, shake hands or pluck hair, spat at us in the distance, laughing and shouting, "Mzungu, Mzungu, Mzungu," and many of them were hugging our legs. With the help of three teachers, it took us more than fifteen minutes before continuing our walk.

One night, the missionary sisters of the Consolata congregation, who worked in the hospital, invited us to dinner in their small and very simple convent. Like good Africans, they sang and danced with us. They all wanted to dance with me, from the director to the oldest one. When I say all, it was because there were about twenty-eight to thirty sisters.

In Kenya, there was a super cute custom. When they had guests to the house, who went for the first time, they prepared a cake. After dinner, all those who lived in the house brought it to you, dancing with the cake held high. It was a whole ceremony. It was a symbol that they were giving everything that they were, so as to form a union with the new guests. They all came to where we were sitting, singing: "Kata, kata, kata osiogope, kata," which means: "Cut, cut, cut, without fear, cut." Then each guest cut a piece of the cake with a fork and gave a little piece of cake to each of the people present. Then the person with the highest rank o cut pieces of cake and gave it to each guest in the mouth.

Having the opportunity to observe our missionary friend – who was at St. Massimo Parish in Meru – interacting with the people of the parish was a living manifestation of God in action. Her wisdom and her people skills stole the hearts of everyone who crossed her path. We very much enjoyed observing her in action. Many times we were participants in those actions, and in others we were her partners in crime.

One Sunday there was a celebration of the women of Meru, in which the parish priest blessed them in a solemn mass, and each one of them carried an offering. All the women made their dresses with the same blue fabric with white squares. Scàrves were made from the same cloth, to cover the head. The ceremony lasted between five to six hours. First, all the women, singing and dancing in a procession, entered the church with their offerings. They walked through the center of the church, without interrupting the singing or dancing, and left their offerings at the foot of the altar. Our friend was at the front of the group, for two reasons: one to honor her for her work, and the other because she was the only "Mzungu" of Meru. To give you an idea of her fabulous genius and sense of humor, the aforementioned brought a live and kicking goat as an offering, to the altar.

Several weeks later, Carolina and I, along with an occupational therapist, a visiting nurse from Holland and our missionary friend, started the first clinic for patients with neurological problems in the area. Until then, the only specialists in the area of neurology were in the city of Nairobi, which made this a great opportunity for many families. From the idea to the execution, it took less than a week. We arrived at the small dispensary where we were going to see patients early one morning. We did not know how many patients would go and if the information about the clinic had been able to reach the people in the surroundings.

Upon arrival, there was some misinformation, and there was no room for us inside the small dispensary. About a hundred meters from where we were, there was an abandoned building. It had walls of concrete brick blocks, as well as a zinc roof and concrete floors. We went in to see, and we were able to remove the debris and leave a space of about four by five meters, where we could see the patients.

Patients could wait outside and pass one at a time. We went to the dispensary and got two wooden benches and five plastic chairs. At the back we found a metal stretcher and a small, wooden table. They lent us a mat from the dispensary. Together, in less than half an hour, we were opening the neurological clinic for the first time.

The occupational therapist was by my side, translating and taking notes of the patients, of the diagnoses we made and of the therapeutic measures we designed. The people were talking mainly local dialects. In five hours we were able to see twenty-five patients, all children under ten years of of age, except for two adolescents aged fifteen years. Ninety percent of the cases had perinatal neurological injury syndromes and infantile cerebral palsy of various types. It was an incredible experience that was filled with a lot of spirituality and missionary content. For me, as a pediatric neurologist, it was a fabulous great opportunity to help, but for the rest of the team it was the first time that they were in direct contact with those types of patients and with their mothers who took them. For

Carolina, this was the first time that she saw myself examining patients directly.

In the manuscript that Carolina wrote, recounting her experiences as a missionary – My Awakening as a Missionary – and which has been the most important source of information that I have had in the writing of these last two chapters, she said verbatim:

'It is the first time that I see Enrique as a doctor working with children. It was super beautiful to see him, how sweet, how affectionate, how delicate. It did not matter the physical condition or cleanliness of the child or the mother. With his hands, with his look, with his smile, he gave them the best of himself. It was really a unique experience that will be marked in my heart for life. They were quite difficult cases, not only children with cerebral palsy, but also malnourished. None of them had been seen by a specialist or received any type of physical therapy. Many were totally contracted, without any flexibility in the joints and with an exaggerated muscle tone. As a family was seen, the rest of the people spread the word that we were there, and more and more mothers began to arrive with their children in tow. It was a life experience that cannot be described in words.

'We agreed that every Wednesday we would go to that place to carry out our duties. Our experience in teaching mothers and children to perform the exercises that Enrique was indicating, turned us, for many hours, into missionary doctors.'

The beautiful rose that we had been enjoying began to drive its thorns into us, while it began to lose its petals.

Every day that passed, it became more and more obvious to us the power that some of the priests who were in contact with us had; where the bureaucracy had kidnapped them, where they sometimes were forgetting the most needy, where vanity dominated their thinking and their feelings, and the pretend to be more was a goal to achieve on a daily basis. In some cases, they did not respect the time of others at all, just to demonstrate their superiority. They could leave people waiting for two or three hours before seeing them.

One morning, to give you an example, they cut down a mango tree to the level of leaving only the main trunk without branches. It was about 100 years old and covered an area of forty meters in diameter. It was a beautiful and spectacular tree, a symbol of the Consolata congregation, planted by the missionaries who built the hospital, and where dozens of families spent the day under its shadow, waiting to be treated or when they went to visit their sick relatives. It was quite a tradition, and it gave large quantities of mangoes twice a year. It was cut off by the vanity of one of the priests, so that a construction that was being carried out nearby would not be disturbed by the people. For Carolina, that thorn stuck in the center of her heart.

Carolina came home today with a lot of mixed feelings. She went to visit the school where they told her that she could work, which was next to the hospital. The director was happy that Carolina went. She knew the facilities and the classrooms. There were about fifty little children per class with a teacher, all the children sitting at their own desks. The ages of the first grades were three to four years old. There was a large blackboard where they wrote the class of the day, and the children copied it in their notebooks.

The little children, happy to see her, sang songs to her, and Carolina took the opportunity and shook hands, one by one, with the whole class and in all the classrooms that she went to. She told me that both the children, the teachers and the principal were positively surprised by the gesture of shaking hands with each student, as it was something they had never seen.

The director introduced Carolina to the staff in the room where the teachers met to have tea, which is a custom there in Africa. Around ten a.m., people and workers stopped their activities to have a tea and eat something. There were about fifteen teachers, sitting with their backs to the wall, watching her. When he had finished introducing her, there was no response from any of them. The director later apologized to Carolina and explained that they feared she might endanger their job. He told her that everything depended on the priest in charge of the hospital, and that as soon as she had the work permits, she could start. As soon as she left the school, she went to talk to the priest, who made her wait for more than three hours before talking to her.

The priest commented to her, to her surprise, that he had not yet sent my papers to Nairobi for the approval of the Medical License necessary so that I could directly prescribe medications. He said that he wanted to do the paperwork personally, and he did not know if he would go to Nairobi in a week or two. So the diocese of Meru had not done anything regarding our work permits. Without those permissions, we were both totally at the disposal of the priest, who literally was doing what he wanted with us. They made us feel like puppets on a string.

The next day, when I went to teach the nursing students, to my surprise, no one attended. I tried to find out what had happened, but the students were avoiding me. Several of the students approached me when I was leaving nursing school and told me, quickly and fearful of being seen, that the director of the hospital forbade them to go to the classes that I gave them. Without understanding exactly what was happening, I decided to go and clarify the situation. The priest in charge made me wait about two hours before talking to me.

In short, he told me that as part of their plans for me in the hospital as a neurology specialist, teaching nurses didn't look good. Before leaving, he let me know that the Infant Cerebral Palsy clinic that we just opened was being questioned, because it was free and because priests could not have control of our activities. Our insistence that the clinic had to be free of charge was against the interests of the hospital. Seeing my facial expression, he told me, with a tone that was a bit unpleasant for me at the time, that that clinic generated a lot of finances for them. I preferred not to say anything and went home.

After telling Carolina that night what was happening, she was really very eloquent, and a variety of words with great content of all kinds of emotions came out of her mouth, accompanied by a very versatile body language. She asked until when were we going to continue to allow the priests to do whatever they wanted with us, keeping absolute control of our activities here. Now I understood why there were so many "buts" that we encountered every time we tried to help. In situations like this, I got frustrated and my spirits went down. Being missionaries was more difficult than I had imagined. The incredible thing was that who made it difficult was the man himself, the bureaucracy, the laziness, taking what they have for free. The need was there, the desire to learn from nurses and doctors existed, the desire of children to see further was there, the desire to improve was latent. But it was the same man who stopped everything. And what hurt me the most was that in these cases, the men involved were the Catholic priests, who were in command of the hospital, the diocese and therefore of us. The words that were said to me the other day echoed in my mind: "We feel like beggars, begging on the ground, asking that they please let us help the needy."

I tried to keep control of my emotions so that they did not cloud my thinking and my actions. Do not think that my silence was apathy, submission or uncertainty. My silence, in those moments, was to try to give the maximum of opportunities to Carolina's wishes to be a missionary in Africa, to give opportunities to those who really needed us where we were. It was a difficult silence, but I think it was necessary. I would speak at the moment when my speech would make a difference, and I would act, instead of using words, to express and define my potential actions.

Of course we were both very clear that something was going on. We knew that we were victims of the Catholic behavior of taking away from the parishioners their self-esteem, to make them more dependent on the condition of being controlled and subdued. We were victims, aware that we were not victimized or even influenced by the attempt to victimize us.

After the second neurology clinic, which we had called the Infant Cerebral Palsy Clinic, the dispensary informed us that they had received the order that we should no longer be allowed to use the abandoned construction for the clinic. In a psychological game, we turned the informant around, and she let us know, unintentionally, who the person who issued the order was.

As we were in Meru, we went to the parish of St. Massimo to speak with the parish priest who was the one who had brought us here and who unfortunately was the one who issued the order to cancel the clinic. His excuse was the cost of gasoline from Nkubu to Meru. We tried to find a solution. We told him that if he lent us one of his seven vehicles, we would bear the cost of gasoline. And he denied it to us, despite the fact that three of those vehicles were bought with donations from the organization we belonged to.

To give you a better idea of why the economic situation played an important role, which the priests handled for their benefit, I will tell you one of the many details that the Mission Doctors Association established as part of its rules, so that one can carry out with them a missionary activity for a period of three years: 'We are allocated the equivalent in local currency of US $50 per month, per person, for our food expenses, etc.'

The priests who were in charge of us knew this very well, and that is why it was very easy for them to think that, with that detail, they could have us dominated. What I think they had obviated was that they were totally wrong about us. We had been going with the flow, giving time for our missionary commitment to succeed, on our standards of what missionary success meant.

On our return to Nkubu, Carolina was removed from the work that she was doing at the Comprehensive Care Center and was told that if she wanted to help, she could work filling little bags with grains. Those bags were the ones that were given to patients. In the nobility and human quality of Carolina, seeing that she could not continue with what she was collaborating with, with pride and humility she began to help every day, in a wooden warehouse where the donated bags of grains were found, to fill sachets with different grains. It was not easy for her, but nevertheless she did it with joy and enthusiasm. I tried to pass as often as I could where she was. Her personality and character were manifesting themselves in a fascinating way, involving everyone who passed by. Within a few days, she already had assistants. People helped her just to spend time with her, chatting and laughing. For me, seeing her reduced to that missionary activity was very difficult to accept.

Meanwhile, the felling of trees of all kinds in the hospital area were aggravating our emotional tolerance. It was not easy to inject our energy in view of all those events.

The day after our arrival from Meru, Carolina and I met two cardiovascular surgeons and an Italian cardiologist, from the city of Milan, who had brought their cardiac monitoring equipment, echocardiogram, stress-test equipment and surgical equipment to do heart valve and coronary artery surgeries. They came for five days. That was the third time they had come. They had been in for two days, and they had only seen four patients a day. They were frustrated and with the Italian blood gushing through the pores of their skin. Supposedly they had been contacted through emails and phone calls long before the current hospital managers, who were different from those in charge for many years and who were part of the Consolata congregation. In previous years, they saw around eighty patients a day. Their main complaint was that nobody was responsible.

I identified so much with their frustration that I decided to help them, without involving those in charge of the hospital and without asking anyone for permission. The four of us toured the hospital and visited all the patients it had, looking for candidates. We went to the outpatient clinic and instructed the nurses and clinical officers to notify us if patients arrived who met the requirements that we explained to them. We managed to get thirty-six patients in the two days they had left in the hospital. There was mutual satisfaction, although the expectations generated prior to their visit were not met. For two days we formed a work team that generated professional satisfaction, while generating a friendship and a sensation of solidarity.

Two days later, Carolina and I got malaria, despite taking daily prophylaxis. We tried to stay active as much as possible. After several days, we recovered our health and began to mobilize ourselves by walking to farther places from Nkubu, in search of something, without knowing what that something would be. Every time we went from Nkubu to Meru, we crossed the equator line.

A project that we had been developing since we arrived in Nkubu with our missionary friend, which consisted of visiting the inmates of the Nkubu prison twice a week, was canceled the first day we were going to start it. At the gate of the jail, after having all the necessary permits and authorizations, the guard told us that we could not enter because of superior orders. After inquiring with the authorities and the bishop of the region, we found out that the order came from the bishop at the request of the priests in charge of the hospital.

Our missionary friend from Meru, along with Carolina and I, began to explore the surroundings, looking for orphanages that we could help with. Since our arrival, there was a constant refusal to inform us about it, since it was forbidden for us to have any kind of connections other than the corresponding ones with the hospital. But at this point, we no longer had any trust with those in charge of the hospital or with the organization to which we belonged, due to their complicity and indolence in what they were trying to do that would mark our realities.

The sisters from the Consolata convent, who invited us to dinner one night, became our accomplices. Apparently the power of the priests was keeping them totally under the yoke of their will. These sisters ran two orphanages, but they were not allowed to tell us about it. There was an expression of freedom on their faces when they gave us the information on where they were located.

We walked with the sister in charge of the first orphanage, who was only a couple of kilometers from the hospital. It was an orphanage for children with special abilities. It consisted of a house built in the shape of an L," with two rooms, about four meters by three meters each. Each room had four bunk beds, with two beds each, with its corresponding bathroom. One room was for boys, and the other for girls. It had a kitchen and a dining room that was also used as a room for studying and playing, as well as for physical therapy, approximately five meters by four meters. In front of the rooms, less than two meters away, there was a chicken coop with several roosters and many chickens that provided them with eggs. In the small garden in front of the building, they had a cow from which they took the milk they drank every day. In the rest of the three-meter-by-three-meter garden, they had some vegetables planted. In total, there were eighteen children. The sister's work was impressive. She was a mother, a teacher, a therapist, a cook, milked the cow, etc. The affection with which she treated the children was a mixture of love and spirituality. It was beautiful to watch her. From then on, we went two to three times a week, mainly to play with the children and to help with physical therapies and meals.

The next orphanage we found was founded by an Italian man named Danielle. The place was amazing. It housed sixty children. The physical structure very well maintained. It started in 2007, with the help of the Mission Consolata in Italy. There were two rooms. Each room had fifteen to sixteen bunk beds, with two or three beds each. Everything was very neat and clean. At the foot of the bunks were one or two trunks, where they kept their clothes and personal things. The girls' room and the boys' room were very similar. By the time we were there, they were building a new room to place the boys under six years of age. There was a fairly large kitchen, a dining room, a garden with cows, chickens, plantings of vegetables, banana trees, etc., in addition to having other large areas of land where they planted corn. The children went to nearby schools and participated in the activities of the parish.

Danielle, in an incredible way, had been building and providing help for the growth of the place and the parish. He built a carpentry shop and, by then, thanks to a donation from some Italian friends, they were making high-quality wooden furniture that they later sold in Nairobi. By the time we went, they had trained seventeen of the older boys to help him in the carpentry.

The orphanage was built in a mountainous area about twenty kilometers from Nkubu. Fresh water came from the mountain, which through filters that they created with stones and some pipe connections, carried that water to the parish, and they planned to take it to the orphanage. They were using hydroelectric power, thus saving on electricity consumption.

We arrived mid-morning on a Saturday, walking and using motorcycle-taxis in some sections. They invited us to lunch with all the children. It was fascinating to enjoy their education when they were talking, in their way of eating, in their respect for the moment, for the food... it was a lovely experience. That orphanage did not belong to the diocese. It was Catholic but private.

The next day, we went early to visit a third orphanage run by two Consolata sisters. It was moving to come into contact with the sixty to seventy children who were living there. It was a mixture of tenderness, innocence, childish joy, and loneliness. We literally felt like our hearts were snuggled. There were more than fifteen of those children who were under one year old. It was a lot of work for those two sisters who were in charge of it. They had very little staff to help them with cooking, gardening, maintenance and taking care of the children.

The children were fascinated to see us, and the sisters were happy with the idea that we had gone to visit them.

When she showed us the chapel, she told us: "This is where we come every morning to ask for strength to start and end the day."

We left the orphanage at the end of the afternoon, with our minds and hearts working on generating possibilities to help them.

Our missionary friend asked us to accompany her to ask the priest in charge of the St. Massimo parish, where she was assigned, that due to the little work that was in the parish, if he could "lend" her to the orphanage; that is, spend a few days at the orphanage and a few days at St. Massimo. The priest, without thinking for a second, gave her a sharp "no." He also threatened her, saying that if she wanted to do that, then she should go live in the orphanage completely.

She tried to contact the organization to help her, but it opportunely played deaf, and for days they left our friend in limbo. Knowing how difficult it was to be living all the time in the orphanage, that much-loved and brave friend made the decision for herself and moved to the orphanage. Carolina and I collaborate with her and the orphanage as much as possible. Distance and lack of transportation were our enemies to overcome. On weekends, she used to go to our little house in Nkubu, and between conversations and a few beers she was able to drain and recharge.

In the following weeks, we spent as much time as possible sharing and helping in the three orphanages.

In one of the trips to one of the orphanages that was quite far away, due to the impossibility of getting transportation, Carolina and I decided to walk. It took us about two hours to get to the parish near the orphanage. Between the fatigue, the thirst and the instincts, we decided to go in and ask about two priests whom we were told were Spaniards. We rang the bell and the door several times, but only a continuous silence was the answer obtained, and when we started to leave, one of the priest arrived in his car. It was Father Gumersindo, originally from Burgos, Spain. He had lived in Africa for forty-three years – seven years in Uganda and the rest in different parts of Kenya.

We greatly enjoyed the conversation in Spanish. The priest was very intelligent, cultured, knowledgeable, studious, friendly, and attentive. Without any desire for arrogance on our part, it was fabulous to have, as they say, a smart conversation. The priest was quite a character, and he had an extraordinary Spanish flavor. He told us about his arrival in Africa at the age of twenty-four. He was about one meter and sixty centimeters tall. He hadn't cut his hair or beard for over ten years. We could say that he was the typical missionary of the movies and stories.

Among his many comments, there was one in particular that Carolina liked a lot, since it identified with what she had been feeling.

He told us: "When you come to the African continent and you are white, you have to go to missions led by whites, because they understand well the connotation of the concept of work for foreigners. For Africans, in the vast majority, working is going to a place from eight in the morning to five in the afternoon and being there, even if they are not doing anything. The white, or those who come from Europe and America, have a different vision of what work is and can get frustrated. For Africans, the work of whites in Africa is limited to giving them donations, giving them money or that they look for money for them. "

Two days before that visit, we had started again with symptoms of malaria, despite the repellants and mosquito nets. We had not stopped taking the prophylactic treatment. The prophylaxis we were taking contained mefloquine hydrochloride, which made it impossible for us to take quinine or chloroquine, which were the two medications that could be obtained in the hospital. We had the option of taking artemisia, if the malaria got complicated. The symptoms that we suffered at that time consisted mainly of tiredness, headaches, fever, stomach pain, nausea, cold sweats, tremors, loss of appetite, and chills. Those malaria symptoms not only weakened us physically, but they were also draining us emotionally.

The next day, Carolina went with the construction engineer to see a new wing of the hospital, which was forbidden to enter and was guarded day and night. That Italian builder was not only in charge of the construction, but also of handling all the funds that came from Italy. As they walked to the construction area, he commented to Carolina that it was very difficult to change the way the African thinks and acts. He did not understand why we were living in the conditions in which we lived and going through so many predicaments. He said it was not only in Kenya, but in other countries in Africa where he had been, when people came to help, that it was mainly to work for the Africans, but they all lived as they did in their respective countries, with the necessary comforts.

In his long experience, he told Carolina that all the missionaries who had come to Africa had had an economic income that allowed them to help, and at the same time had a vehicle to transport themselves, money to pay for gasoline, their meals and housing provided, etc. He told Carolina that it was totally contradictory to be in the conditions we were in and that he really didn't know how to classify us.

In the middle of that conversation, they arrived at the new construction. He told her that the new construction was done with money from donations sent to improve the quality of patient care. But those in charge of the hospital decided to build a private area for the exclusive use of people with high purchasing power. They called it the VIP hospital. It had state-of-the-art plasma televisions installed in each room. There were twelve rooms in total. Each of them had electric clinical beds brought from Europe and intensive-care equipment. There was a satellite dish only for that wing of the hospital. The mattresses on the beds were specially brought from Italy. It had its own nursing station, as well as its own kitchen and laundry. The builder explained to Carolina that according to the priests in charge, it would be very lucrative, and with that money they would help other areas of the hospital.

Carolina came home that afternoon, saying that such a grotesque incongruity was impossible to be explained; that it was an impudence; how could they build something like that in a missionary hospital where there were so many deficiencies; what superficiality and what a wrong idea of what medicine was.

It was not easy to sleep that night, despite the several beers that were introduced into our bodies amid the stormy debate of such mixed feelings.

Two days later and still symptomatic with malaria, we attended a funeral for one of the sisters from the Consolata congregation. The funeral began at eight a.m. in the mortuary of the hospital, with approximately sixty sisters from various congregations, plus friends and family. A priest blessed the deceased sister, as well as those present. While the people and priests said the corresponding prayers, the group of sisters were singing. The deceased was placed in a room. All of us passed by to see it. Carolina and I stayed in a corner, where we were not interrupting the passage of the mourners, in order to better observe the details of that part of the ceremony. The vast majority of people were taking pictures of her or filming her with small cameras.

The smell was quite strong, since almost three days had passed since the death, and since there was no refrigeration in the hospital, they kept her in a tank with formaldehyde. After everyone present came to see her, she was carried in a procession to her hearse. Many cars and buses were packed with people to accompany her to the sisters' cemetery, about an hour away. The cemetery was next to one of the orphanages we visited. Personnel from the diocese filmed her funeral, with all the details around her. The sisters were the ones who carried the urn at all times.

We arrived at the cemetery and first entered the sisters' chapel. There they sang and prayed to her and then carried her to the parish church where the bishop was waiting, while all sisters sang to her constantly. It was a great ceremony, with sixty priests and approximately two hundred sisters from different congregations, plus family and friends.

The mass began at ten a.m. and ended at three thirty in the afternoon, then the deceased sister was taken in procession to the cemetery. The other sisters were singing all the time, as well as the friends and relatives present. Once the urn was lowered, all those present, one by one, grabbed a fist of earth and threw it towards the urn. When all those present had already passed, the men and some women of the local government alternated so that, with a shovel, filled the grave with earth until it was completely covered.

At the end of that ceremony, the bishop slowly approached, carrying a wooden cross that had the sister's name carved on it. Upon reaching the grave, he buried it at the head. Later, the bishop walked to where the mountain of flower crowns was, took one and placed it next to the cross. Subsequently, the bishop called, from a list that he had, the representatives of organizations, close relatives and the medical and administrative staff of the hospital, and each one placed a wreath on the grave. Later, all those who were present approached, and from the tables around, that contained plants and flowers in small pots, took one and planted it on and around the tomb. Then everyone went to a dining room in the diocese, which was nearby, to eat. There would be about three hundred people eating.

The next day, Carolina and I left early in the morning and walked to the Mission of the Spanish priests. When we arrived, there were the two priests, Father Gumersindo and the other father, whose name was Enrique. The welcome from both of them was very pleasant. We had a very nice conversation. Once again, we were able to enjoy what the idea of being a missionary father was for us. Both were simple people, hardworking, with a lot of human quality, concerned about others, and waiting to help.

After a couple of hours, we went with Father Gumersindo to see one of the churches – or houses of prayer – that belonged to the parish. In total, there were twenty-two houses of prayer. He explained to us that in Kenya, as there are many villages, the way the Christian religion had spread was by creating houses of prayer in each village. Those houses of prayer were small churches where the parishioners gathered on Sundays. Since there weren't enough priests to celebrate Mass every Sunday in each house of prayer, one person was assigned to act as a deacon. Thus, the fathers visited a different chapel every Sunday to celebrate Mass. The father told us that in their parish, there were still houses of prayer that met under the shade of the trees.

Later, we went to visit a boy who suffered from a hereditary degenerative muscle disease. The mother had had three children, and all three had suffered from the same disease; two had already died. Her had husband left her as soon as he learned that her third child also suffered from the disease. The mother lived alone with her son, whom she had to watch almost constantly.

They lived in a small house measuring two meters by 1.5 meters, with cardboard walls and wooden boards, a dirt floor and a zinc roof, with two cots and a small plot of five meters by five meters, where they planted vegetables. The boy was fifteen years old. It was about four years since he had lost the ability to walk and stand. The missionary father told us that the boy was deteriorating rapidly. We stayed with the mother and the boy for a long time, explaining what they could do to facilitate their ambulation, and we built them, with what we found in the surroundings, parallel bars for their ambulation in the little house and in the surroundings, as well as handles with pulleys and ropes that helped him to move on a kind of skateboard with rollers.

After several hours, we went to visit a group of sisters who were in charge of a dispensary and a school. For Carolina and me, it was literally transporting ourselves to another dimension –to the dimension that we were wanting to be in Africa as missionaries. It was truly a gift from the divinity of creation. We felt like the day lasted sixty hours. It was a beautiful thing. We were experiencing the other side of the coin of being missionaries. We had met missionaries of conviction, missionaries who were putting their hearts, souls and minds to help and give love to all human beings who were in their life paths.

On the way back, the father dropped us off near Nkubu, since it was nighttime. We still walked another half hour. During our walk, Carolina told me that it was not easy for her to be there; that when we decided to be missionaries, she knew that it was going to cost us a lot to adapt to this new situation, but she always thought that the difficult part would be experiencing poverty up close, to be exhausted from trying so hard to give every day, to stay exhausted from our daily work side by side with the locals, leaving the house and spending all day collaborating with those in need. She thought it would be difficult to be able to have free time, to be able to rest, and difficult to have time free even to communicate with our loved ones, etc.

She never imagined that she would spend her days in a very rudimentary little house, waiting to be allowed to do things. She never imagined that her only activity would be one or two hours a day. She never imagined that she would not have direct contact with the town or with the people. She never imagined that she was going to feel like a missionary without mission. With tears in her eyes, she told me that she had never prepared for what she was experiencing.

She told me that she was constantly questioning whether she was doing the right thing, especially when she saw that she was doing almost nothing all day where she was, where she saw that there was so much need around which she was not allowed to help with or was blocked from participating, where our main intention was to give, to be able to share, to be able to help, to be able to learn, to be able to become one of the community, sharing with them their vicissitudes and trying to alleviate their weight.

She began to question if she should continue there, if she should continue sacrificing being so far from the family to spend the day there in the house just sitting. She wondered if it was worth the sacrifice of not seeing our parents, our son, our Rony, our brothers, our friends. She wondered if we were rather sacrificing those who we were helping so much around us, as we did before coming to Africa, to be sitting there in that house. She was questioning herself, because where we were before we came, we were helping our neighbor much more than we were helping here.

With her eyes dropping tears, which were like daggers in my heart, she said: "I keep knocking on doors, I keep, and I keep, and I keep…"

She wondered if it was worth feeling that she was slowly wasting away. She said that she had many doubts and that she was very disappointed. She was questioning and questioning and questioning.

She was asking herself if perhaps the only lesson that she had learned as a missionary – and she was reaffirming that we could be missionaries wherever we lived – was that we didn't have to come to Africa to be a missionary. What you had to have was the missionary spirit.

While Carolina stayed at home and bathed, by taking water from a punch bowl with a plastic container, I went to town to buy four beers and something for dinner. When I returned, Carolina was waiting for me outside the house. She told me not to make any decisions yet and that she already felt a little better after the catharsis. We stayed outside, drinking the beers and eating what I had brought.

We said that life, per se, was just a frequency of energy that moved in a sinusoidal way. A few moments of moving up and others of moving down. We were commenting that, in reality, there were no differences, since it was the same energy. It was our interpretations and connotations that defined the up movement as positive and the down movement as negative.

We thought that perhaps we had to get away from the realities we were living in, in order to see the big picture. We decided to let events flow and trust our instincts that were telling us that something was already imminent in what we were living. We didn't know what it was, but we decided to trust and watch carefully. I think that the physical and emotional fatigue, accompanied by the two beers that we each drank, interfered in the decision to leave everything as it was.

That night it started to rain heavily, and it did not stop raining for the next two days. The entire area we were in was flooded. Roads and roads were impassable. We stayed for those days in the hospital area. Carolina was able to help for several hours at the Comprehensive Care Center. The nurses were sick. For Carolina, it was very positive. She felt useful, and that encouraged her to continue fighting.

All those experiences, so full of joy, satisfaction, conflicting emotions, confused feelings, thoughts moving between reason and intelligence, laughter and tears, frustrations and unexpected realities, since our arrival on this continent, has allowed me to identify one of the secrets hidden in the missionary intent – I speak of the simplicity. Africa had been trying to teach us that no effort was ever wasted, although it was not easy to see its dividends in the midst of so many basic needs. Simplicity sometimes gave the false idea of wasting time, until people's eyes and smiles told us otherwise. In all this, the intentions of a greater good were hidden and difficult to identify.

Africa was becoming for us a life experience that swayed between what it was and what we wanted it to be, between the beauty of its people and the malice of its exceptions, between the simplicity and the divinity.

One night at around seven p.m., Father George knocked on the door of the house where we were living. He was a missionary priest originally from India, who lived about six kilometers away from Nkubu. We had seen him once at one of the ceremonial masses. We talked about all kinds of topics, from philosophy, theology, the need for religion, the different religions in India, the difference between what it was to be Catholic in India and what it was to be Catholic in other countries of the world, etc.

Regarding the latter, he told us that in most other countries, one is Catholic because he "believes" first. In India, due to his ancestral roots and deep-rooted culture, first one questions oneself, wonders, meditates and then believes.

He had been talking for almost two hours, and we still didn't know why he had come to visit us. Between the lines, it seemed like he wanted something from us, but he couldn't quite figure out how to ask us. In the middle of the conversation, I asked him how he wanted us to do what he was asking us to do.

He stared at us and said with enthusiasm: "I want you to come to my parish and give a talk to the parishioners about HIV and AIDS."

Carolina and I looked into each other's eyes and laughed, while simultaneously saying that of course we would, with great pleasure. After asking him when this would happen, he answered us clearly and concisely: "Tomorrow morning." Minutes later, he left.

We left very early the next morning, walking towards the parish by climbing the Kenia mountain. Its mountainous and cold climate made the walk a pleasant walk. On arrival, we found that there were a large number of parishioners.

Bearing in mind that the father wanted me to speak only about HIV and AIDS, I began by highlighting the importance of educated information in prevention, of the concept of family in the commitment of shared love, and of believing out of conviction and not out of submission. After about twenty minutes of focusing on those topics, they began to ask questions, which led us to talk about diagnosis, prognoses, direct prevention, sex, personal hygiene, customs, culture, spirituality, quality of life, love, death, euthanasia, beliefs, commitment to the partner, to the family, to the children, etc.

The talk lasted about three hours. It was fascinating to be part of the interest and hunger for information of so many people. During the talk, I checked on what the father who invited us had told us. The parish was very active, but not very believing. Future talks on a variety of other topics were pending.

On our return to Nkubu, we found our fellow missionary from St. Massimo, waiting for us at the door. She was so angry that she literally seemed to be fuming and sparking. Between her frustration and feeling cheated, and between tears of pain and anger, she told us that since she had managed the finances of the parish where she was, she had calculated that maintaining the Cerebral Palsy Clinic had cost about seventy-five dollars a month.

She told us that for several days before starting the clinic, she was discussing it with her missionary friend that had to return to the United States two months after her arrival to Kenya. Since then, she had begun sending the pastor of St Massimo $200 a month to help the clinic succeed and continue to grow. That missionary friend, in the distance, again relived unpleasant experiences around the figure of the parish priest, which played an important role in having left her mission in Africa. She was left in a furious shock when she learned that the clinic had been canceled for being very expensive, and because there was no money.

The volcanoes of mixed emotions of those two missionary colleagues and friends caused the contained volcano of Carolina to erupt. That night, our friend smoked like an erupting volcano and drank beers until she managed to cool the burning lava. Carolina and I did not accompany her with the smoking, but we went along with the beers. It was a long, emotionally draining night. The mixture of fatigue and beers allowed us to sleep for a few hours, almost at dawn.

Days later, Carolina and I walked towards the parish of Father George. It was about two hours of walking to get there and another two or more to return, since the way down was more difficult. When we arrived, the father was not there, so we turned around and began to walk back. While we were enjoying the beautiful scenery, we met a large number of children, always laughing and greeting us in their style. Part of the way, Carolina and I discussed our stay in Kenya again, going over the pros and cons.

When we got home, we found an e-mail from our son Ricardo, telling us that he was coming from Manhattan in a few days to spend Christmas with us. The news revolutionized our thinking and our feelings.

Ricardo's arrival illuminated every cell of our bodies. The three of us shared unforgettable moments as a family. We met and enjoyed certain touristy parts of the area, including a safari. We had unique experiences watching Ricardo mix with so much love with the children in the orphanages and with the local people. Ricardo brought suitcases full of new clothes and toys for the children, as well as some cash from donations from coworkers and friends in Manhattan. With the money, he bought sacks of food for the orphanages. He also bought sixty mattresses for the wooden beds of one of the orphanages. He gave the children the new clothes and toys, in coordination with the sisters. He engendered happiness, joy, and hope. He spoke with the adolescents to fill them with alternatives for improvement.

The children of the largest orphanage, where they received the new clothes, held a mass with all of them to give thanks for the gifts they had received. The arrival of boys, girls and male and female adolescents, who entered the church wearing the things that Ricardo had brought them, generated an explosion of laughter and tears in all three. They all wore their clothes with the tags on the outside.

The sister in charge approached us, very excited, and whispered in our ears: "They are happy, since it is the first time in their life that they wear new clothes, and that is why they are very proud and puffed up, showing the labels."

At the end of December, Ricardo returned to Manhattan. After his return to Manhattan, he maintained contact with many of the adolescents for years.

Days of a lot of thinking and analyzing feelings came with Ricardo's departure. Walking with Carolina through the hospital areas on New Year's Day, we entered the VIP construction that was already finished. There was one of the clinical officers who was going to work there. He greeted us with great enthusiasm, as he told us that it was a great pleasure and a great opportunity to learn, working as part of my medical team. He told us about the whole project. He show us the publicity that they were going to start doing in the first days of January. Carolina and I were speechless after hearing every word he said. He showed us how much they were going to charge for neurology outpatient visits – US $80. They announced that the VIP clinic-hospitalization was going to be directed by a neurologist who was certified by the American Board of Neurology and Psychiatry, with my photo next to the writing, etc.

After saying goodbye to the enthusiastic doctor, we walked back to the house. We did not speak a single word to each other. Carolina organized the minimum clothing we needed to travel, and we decided to go and talk to the sister in charge of the orphanages.

We spoke with the sister of the details and the logistics of taking all our belongings that were in the house for her orphanages, before the parents in charge of the hospital prevented her, as they had already done on multiple occasions. We literally left toothbrushes, shoes, watches, ninety-five percent of our clothes, food, all utensils, mosquito nets, water filters, clothes, medical equipment, etc.

Carolina coordinated the logistics of the return trip, and in a few days we were leaving via Caracas, Venezuela.

One of the most important lessons of all these missionary adventures was having understood that fear is our greatest enemy, not only in finding the divinity that is in us, but in being able to manifest love in all the potential that we feel it.

Fear also slows down our walk through life, weakens our passions, and fills us with uncertainties and insecurities that make it almost impossible to achieve the goals we set for ourselves. If we learn to identify fear and its manifestations, insinuations and camouflages, we will have learned to be the creators of our realities.

Fear is not just fear. Fear is the quicksand of our lives. When we are submerged in the quicksand of fear, only the control of our emotions will allow us to generate the appropriate thoughts that will forge the necessary actions; not to continue being sucked, but to get out of it.

Habits and customs are our worst enemies in this regard. We become accustomed to living in fear, making it part of our customs, and over time we only seek to be able to breathe better, while we are submerged up to our noses in the swamp.

In this way, our happiness and quality of life are limited to the ability to breathe well, while we are up to our noses with all our limitations.

Unfortunately, no one will come to get us out of the quicksand pit we've gotten ourselves into. It is in us, and only in us, to avoid continuing to be sucked, and to get out of those realities in order to have the freedom to exercise our free will, in the four directions of the wind, in the process of creating our earthly realities.

As a doctor I was able to verify, once again, that no matter where you are in the world or what socioeconomic position you experience, you will never achieve the healing or cure of any physical, mental or emotional illness while living submerged in the quicksand of the fear.

Without fear, allopathic medicine and homeopathic medicine are leveled. Temporary and circumstantial fear is necessary as a survival mechanism. I speak of chronic fear, of that fear that invades our thinking, our feelings, our actions and our talking on a daily basis. I speak of that fear that robs us of the executive functions of personality, character and memory of our frontal brain lobe, by redistributing blood volume towards our primitive brain component involved in survival, simultaneously decreasing our immune response.

Healing or cure has nothing to do with the remedies, but with consciousness.

The programs of our mind and heart are not permanent, but on the contrary, constantly changing in essence. Life is, per se, a constant change. Getting stuck in what we were prevents us from knowing and enjoying who we are. If we do not know or enjoy who we are, what we create for our future will simply be more of the same.

When we live trapped in the clutches of fear, we confuse what Albert Einstein said: 'Imagination is more important than knowledge.' And we begin to create our knowledge based on our imagination, which is totally contaminated with the multifaceted connotations of fear.

Fear is not something that we see or feel on a day-to-day basis. Fear, when present in our daily lives, becomes the grand master of the orchestra of our memories deposited in our subconscious, which is what determines ninety-five percent of our actions.

As long as we do not control our fears, our actions will not change, although we believe that working five percent of our actions controlled by our consciousness, will make us find the realities that we are looking for in our lives.

The saddest thing is that fear, per se, does not exist, only the fearful attitudes that we create ourselves, among our emotional, existential, spiritual and cognitive weaknesses. Everything is and only is. Our perception, trained by our beliefs, by their connotations and their interpretations, is what decides to interpret reality as fearful or not. The reality, per se, remains the same.

I have learned to accept my realities without reacting to them. I no longer determine my future by taking into account the learnings of my past. I have already let go, with gratitude, all the teachings that I have received throughout my life from my parents, friends, family, schools, and religion.

In order to be what I am in this new consciousness, I need to stop being what I was, what was created in me, what I lived, what grew in me and in all those who shared with me, and everything that I have projected in a consciousness that is dying, and which we have affectionately called the old consciousness. An old consciousness that led the minds of humanity for centuries, swinging between darkness and half-light. The new consciousness of light, by its very essence, dissipates the old consciousness in its path.

Without trying to give an opinion or make judgments on the religions and their parishioners, I learned that religion is looking for the divinity of creation within the little wooden box where we have our earthly reality locked up. Religion makes us like a fish living in a tank, which, according to the intensity with which we participate in it, gives us the impression that the tank is bigger and more important, or failing that, smaller and insignificant. Religions are crystal fish tanks submerged in the ocean of spirituality, making us believe that because we see the potential of spirituality through the glass of their respective dogmas, we experience it in all its essence and immensity. When we break the crystal of our fishbowl-religion, we can say that we are using, without deceiving ourselves, our free will to explore, not only the wonders and beauties of the ocean of spirituality, but of all the unimaginable places where it can lead us.

In this learning process, the most beautiful and enriching thing is being able to have had the opportunity to enjoy the respect for the diversity. We all have our moments, and the important thing is that we enjoy them with all the intensity that our thinking and our feelings are capable of. It does not matter that we live in a wooden box or in all of nature simultaneously. It does not matter that we live in a fish tank or in the ocean. All the alternatives are wonderful and unique in their essences. The important thing is not to feel that we are more or less than another, because of the place we have chosen or where life has placed us. Our place is our divinity, our God, our mission and the source of our love, our happiness and our joy. Let us enjoy, with the best of our thinking, our feelings, our actions and our speaking, who we are and what we have. Everything is just a moment, and life is full of moments.

I have also let go, blessing it, all that I consciously believe that I have learned. I respect the opinions of others about me and my actions, without allowing them to play any role in the way I use my free will.

I believe that life handles our existential, emotional and spiritual growth like a dance – two steps forward and one step back; one step forward and two steps back – leaving us with the feeling that we are stagnant.

I have the feeling that the experience of earthly life perhaps is not about the humans, per se, but it is an experience that the divinity of creation has designed, so that through free will, Gaia, light and darkness are invented and reinvented.

My instinct tells me that the manifestation of darkness in our humanity has reached the zero point of its sinusoidal sequence, to begin to ascend to its counterpart, the enlightenment. We will continue to be as human as we are, but in the light and with so much illumination. We will not be able to differentiate between what is divine and what is human, since we will not notice the difference.

I believe that now I will be able to be a missionary with a mission. Thank you.